Hebridean Dance

Dannsa nan Eileanach

Hebridean Dance

Dannsa nan Eileanach

Còmhlan Dannsa nan Eileanach

acair

The publishers acknowledge subsidy from the Scottish Arts Council for the publication of this volume.

First published in Scotland in 1995 by Acair Ltd, 7 James Street, Stornoway, Isle of Lewis

© 1995 Còmhlan Dannsa nan Eileanach
© Front cover photograph Donald Ferguson
© Photographs Jon Paul

Dances transcribed by Mats Melin

Designed and typeset by Acair Ltd.
Printed by Stornoway Gazette, Stornoway, Lewis

ISBN 0 86152 913 8

A book of
Hebridean Dance
as performed today on
the Isle of Barra.

Described by
Ceitidh Anna NicFhionghuin
Ceiteag Chaimbeul
Mairead NicNèill
of
Còmhlan Dannsa nan Eileanach

Clàr-innse / Contents

A Modern Dance

Two Traditional Reels

A Modern Reel

ROIMH-RADH

On a thug e toil-inntinn mhòr dhomh pàirt a ghabhail ann an clò-bhualadh an leabhair seo, anns a bheil Dannsa nan Eileanach air an sgrìobhadh le cinnt agus soilleireachd, tha mi fada an comain nan neach a leanas airson an taic a thug iad dhuinn:—Maighistir Cailein MacAonghais a chuidich agus a bhrosnaich sinn gu na dannsaichean ath-nuadhachadh. Fearchar MacNèill agus Ceit Anna NicFhionghuin a rinn mòran rannsachaidh agus sgrùdaidh, Murdina NicNèill, dannsairean Bòrd Dannsa Nan Eileanach, na pìobairean Peadar Forbes agus Seumas MacCormaig a bha aig gach àm cho aontach airson ar cuideachadh; Iain MacAonghais (Iain Pheadair) a chuidich le eachdraidh, Mairead NicNèill a chuidich le cànain. Taing gu h-àraid do Mats Melin às an t-Suain airson na dannsaichean a sgrìobhadh dhuinn cho snasail agus cho inntinneach.

Ceiteag Chaimbeul
(Sgrìobhadair a' chòmhlain)

FOREWORD

Since it gave me great pleasure to take part in the production of this book on authentic Hebridean Dance, acknowledgement goes to the following: Father Colin MacInnes who helped and encouraged us initially to revive the Hebridean Dances. Farquhar MacNeil and Katie Ann MacKinnon who did much research and classification, Murdina MacNeil and the dancers of Bòrd Dannsa Nan Eileanach and pipers Peter Forbes and Seamus MacCormick who were always happy to help in every way, John MacInnes of Daliburgh for historical references, Margaret MacNeil for support in Gaelic language, and last but not least Mats Melin from Sweden, who painstakingly transcribed and arranged the dances for us with such style and elegance.

Katie Campbell
(Group Secretary)

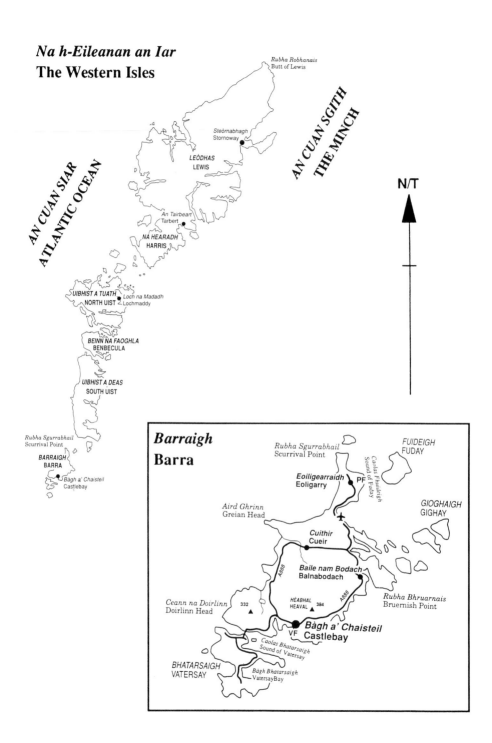

Eachdraidh nan Dannsaichean.

Thàinig na dannsaichean a tha aig làimh san leabhar seo bho Eoghan MacLachlainn. Bhuineadh e do na crìochan mun cuairt air Lochabar — 's dòcha Mòrair no Arasaig. Bhàsaich e ann an taigh Nèill MhicCormaig ann an Dalabrog, Uibhist a Deas, air an dàrna latha deug dhen Iuchar anns a' bhliadhna ochd ceud deug trì fichead 's a naoi-deug (1879) aig aois ceithir fichead bliadhna.

'S e Aonghas MacLachlainn a b' athair dha ach chan eil cinnt air ainm a mhàthar. Bha dà phiuthar aige a bha a' fuireach aig aon àm an Uibhist a Deas. Bhàsaich an tè a b' òige ach phòs an tèile, Iseabail, Dòmhnall MacDhòmhnaill Aonghais à Loch Aineort. B' esan seanair Sheumais Dhòmhnallaich a bha a' còmhnaidh aig croit No. 4. Loch Aineort a Deas, agus sinn-seanair Mhaighstir Iain Aonghais Dhòmhnallaich a tha 'n-dràsd' na Phears'-Eaglais ann an Eaglais Naomh Màiri, An Gearasdan.

Tha e coltach gu robh Eoghan san Fhraing ag ionnsachadh Sagairteachd, agus gu mì-fhortanach ghabh e galair-cnàmh no neo-chomas air choreigin a chrìon a làmh 's a chùm e bho dhreuchd a leantainn. 'S e 'Fear Na Làimhe Bige' a theirte ris an dèidh seo.

Ged a b' fheudar dha a' Cholaisde fhàgail cha do thill e dhachaigh sa mhionaid idir, agus bha amharas gu robh cion airgid air. Tha e ri ràdh gun do thog e air gu siubhal san Fhraing, 's gun robh e a' tathaich Fèisean is Cruinneachaidhean mu Normandy 's mun Bhreatainn Bhig. An seo fhuair e eòlas air dannsaichean-dùthchail agus beul-aithriseach.

A rèir an sgrùdaidh againne thill e a dh'Alba an ceann ùine. Fhuair e obair ann an Sgìre Earra-Ghàidheil na 'Cheistear' ann an Uibhist a Deas. Tha e coltach nach robh tuarasdal idir aige, agus gur ann mar seo a thionndaidh e gu teagasg dannsa airson beò-shlàint'.

Thàinig sinn tarsainn air trì caochladh bheachdan air mar a fhuair e fiosrachadh air na dannsaichean a bha e a' teagasg.

1. Gun do thog e iad air a thuras-siubhail san Fhraing.

2. Gun do thachair e air feadhainn de fhir-leanmhainn a' Phrionnsa Teàrlaich san Fhraing a dh'ionnsaich dha na dannsaichean. (Bha iomradh ann gun do rinn sinn searan na feadhnach-sa suas na Dannsaichean Eileanach.)

3. Gun do rinn e fhèin suas na dannsaichean an dèidh dha thighinn a dh'fhuireach a dh'Uibhist..

'S e 'Gilleasbuig Saor' no Gilleasbuig Mac a' Phearsainn às an Iochdar agus Dòmhnall Dòmhnallach à Dalabrog 'Roidean' an dithis a b' ainmeile dheth na dannsairean aige. Tha fios is cinnt againn gun robh e a' teagasg 'dannsa' ann am Bòrnais cho fad air ais ri ochd ceud deug 's dà fhichead.

Tha iad a-nis air an ainmeachadh 'Dannsaichean nan Eileanach,' mar a mhiannaich Fearchar Eòin Fhearchair à Barraigh — a chionns gur ann sna h-Eileanan an Iar a-mhàin a bha iad air an cleachdadh, ro àm a' Chiad Chogaidh.

Rinn Fearchar, còmhla ri Ceit Anna NicFhionghuin, oidhirp mhòr gu na dannsaichean seo ath-bheothachadh. B' e a sheanair Niall Cannaich (An Clench) a dh'ionnsaich dha iad. An uair mu dheireadh a chunnacas 'An Clench' a' dannsa 's ann an 1938, dà bhliadhna mun do bhàsaich e aig aois ceithir fichead 's a dhà. Dhanns Fearchar e fhèin na dannsaichean seo anns an Albert Hall an Lunnain ann an 1934.

Tha sinn fada nan comain is an comain na feadhnach a leanas:

Gilleasbuig Mac a' Phearsainn, Dòmhnall Dòmhnallach, Iain MacLeòid (Iain Ruadh Phàdraig) à Uibhist a Deas — na dannsairean, Ceit Anna NicFhionghuin, Mona NicNèill (Mona Sheonaidh Màiri) airson an ùidh 's an rùn a bh' aca, 's an dìcheall a rinn iad gus ar dannsaichean a thogail gu inbhe is urram.

Na Dannsaichean

'S e ruidhlichean le dà chupal mar a tha *Cath Nan Coileach*, is *Ruidhle nan Coileach Dhubha*, agus ruidhlichean le ceathrar a bu dual dha na h-Eileannan an Iar, is do thaobh an Iar Alba.

Chailleadh eòlas air an 'Step-Dancing' a bha cho dligheach dhar sinnsirean, agus na àite chaidh dannsaichean aon-neach a stèidheachadh.

B' olc an airidh gun do thachair seo, oir bha iad cho innleachdach air an cuir ri chèile, a' dealbhachadh gnothaichean sònraichte a thachair. Tha fios againn bho bheul-aithris gum biodh feadhainn dhiubh a' comharrachadh gnìomhan a bhuineadh do sheann dòighean creidheamh, toradh na talmhainn, an aimsir, bàs is caithris, leannanachd is pòsadh.

Bha seo cumanta air feadh na Gàidhealtachd agus bhiodh cleachdaidhean gach còmhnaidh ionadail air an dealbhachadh nan dòigh àraid fhèin. 'S e a' phìob-mhòr no puirt-a-beul mar bu trice an ceòl a bhiodh leotha, 's dòcha corra uair an fhidheal.

Thug daoine rinn imrich-cuain a-null thairis leotha an seòrsa dannsa seo. Chùm iad beò iad le bhith gan ionnsachadh dhan cuid chloinne bho linn gu linn. Tuigidh sinn uile gum biodh e nàdarra dhan fhògarrach greimeachadh ri cuimhneachan sam bith air a dhachaigh. Sin mar a thachair. Gu h-annasach 's ann co-cheangailte ri 'Step-Dancing Cheap Bhreatainn' a tha a' chuid as motha dhiubh a' nochdadh, agus a rèir choltais 's ann am Miùghalaigh a bha tùs aig mòran dhiubh.

Ann an Eilean Cheap-Bhreatainn 's e Ruidhlichean Cheithir-làmhan, Ruidhlichean Ochd-làmhan, Dannsaichean Aon-neach, agus fear no dhà de Dhannsa-chleasan Gàidhlig bu mhotha bhiodhte a' cleachdadh. Tha 'stepean' an dannsa aon-neach gu math aonaichte nan cumadh. Tha an dannsair a' dèanamh na steapan air ball 's a' cumail tìm ris a' cheòl le sròn agus sàil na bròige mu seach, le sguabadh beag a-mach 's a-staigh leis a chois. Tha na casan faisg air an làr fad an t-siubhail.

Dancing in the Hebrides

Most of the dances described in this book came, we believe, from one source, namely Ewan MacLachlan, who was born in 1799 and died — a bachelor — in 1879. His father was Angus MacLachlan. Ewan was sometimes referred to as 'Mac Iseabail Rèitalain' which suggests that his mother's name was Isabel and that they came from Retland in Morar. Their home was at croft no 4 South Locheynort in South Uist. Ewan had two sisters – one of whom died young and unmarried. The other sister Isabella married Donald MaDonald (Dòmhnall MacDhòmhnaill 'Ic Iain) in 1830. They moved from Greenock to Locheynort and lived there for the rest of their lives.

It is said that Ewan went to France to study for the Priesthood. Unfortunately, he developed (according to our research) a bone disease or some such disability, which left him with a stunted arm. He was seemingly known in the Islands as 'Fear na Làimhe Bige' (the short-armed man). We are told that although Ewan had to leave College, he did not immediately return to Scotland. Instead, he remained in France and spent a great deal of time going to Festivals around Normandy and Brittany and this is where he probably developed his interest in dancing and folk-lore.

When he evenutally returned to Scotland, we are told that he worked as a Catechist in South Uist. This seemingly was an unpaid job. Ewan turned to dancing as a source of income.

No-one can be absolutely certain as to the origin of our Hebridean Dances, so-called because they were practised only in the Hebrides before the first World War. Ewan's papers were seemingly burned after his death. Some say that he learned his dances in France — others, that, while in France he met some of the followers of Bonnie Prince Charlie, whose ancestors, some believe, made up the dances and that he learned the dances from them. The names of the dances would certainly suggest some connection with the Prince, for example, (*Over the Waters to Charlie* or *Thairis an Aiseig Gu Teàrlach* as it is now known). It is also suggested that Ewan himself made up the dances, influenced by his many visits to the Festivals in France. The only thing we are certain of is that our dances came from Ewan, who taught them in Bornish, in Uist as far back as 1840. Among his pupils were Archibald Macpherson of Iochdar, South Uist and Donald Morrisonls (Roidean) of Daliburgh, South Uist. The South Uist Games Committee held a dancing competition in the early 1920's and interest in the dances was then revived. Archibald and Donald were the only competitors and it seems that the former won the day. They then began to teach the dances locally and it is probably because of this that we can now pass them on to you. These dances probably came to Barra from Ewan himself and also from Ronald Morrison of South Uist, who was married to a girl from Barra. They lived in Barra for some time and he seemingly held a dancing class in Castlebay. One of Archibald Macpherson's best pupils was John MacLeod of Iochdar, South Uist, who did a lot to keep our dances alive. He taught dancing in Uist and Barra. It is from him that Katie Ann Mackinnon of Sgoil Dannsa nan Eileanach got her first steps. He was a relative of her father's, who also came from Uist. John only died a few years ago and is therefore one of our most recent sources.

Fearchar MacNeil of Barra (Patron of Bòrd Dannsa nan Eileanach) lives in Castlebay, Barra and at the age of eighty still remembers the dances and their history. He was taught by his grandfather Neil Buchanan, better known as 'An Clench'. Fearchar remembers seeing him dance in 1938 at the age of eighty, two years before he died. Fearchar displayed some of our dances in the Albert Hall in London in 1934. Fearchar, with the help of Katie Ann Mackinnon has done a great deal to revive the dances which we, in this book, present to you.

Katie Ann was taught most of the dances by Mona MacNeil of Barra, who, with her sister, Nellie, held a dancing class in Castlebay. They were taught by Fearchar! Katie Ann still teaches dancing in Barra and should you need help with these dances you can contact her c/o Còmhlan Dannsa nan Eileanach, Barra or at 'Faire Rhum', 139 Brevig, ISLE OF BARRA.

We sincerely hope that you will enjoy these old dances, as handed down to us by Ewan MacLachlan, a true dancing MASTER, who died at the home of Mr Neil MacCormick, a crofter at Daliburgh, South Uist. It was he who signed the entry in the death register, according to John MacInnes of the Old School House, Daliburgh, South Uist, who was for some time Registrar in South Uist. John was able to give us a lot of information about Ewan, which he himself got from his grandmother Flora Morrison. Some of Ewan's relatives still live in South Uist.

——oOo——

Gluasadan Sònraichte
SPECIAL MOVEMENTS

The terminology in this book follows what is standard in describing Highland and National Dances. The following remarks have been included to clear any doubts of the definitions that have been modified to fit the Hebridean standard of dancing as it is performed today.

In Hebridean dancing the knees are more bent and relaxed than in Highland dancing. All movements should be rhythmic and graceful and should follow with the music.

'Individual interpretation' of these dances are called for as long as the character of the movements/dances stay Hebridean. But on the other hand the steps must be executed accurately.

ABBREVIATIONS:

R = Right
L = Left
RF = Right Foot
LF = Left Foot
RDF = Right Diagonal Front/Forward
RDB = Right Diagonal Back/Backward
LDF = Left Diagonal Front/Forward
LDB = Left Diagonal Back/Backward
Aer. = Aerial
Int. = Intermediate
Pos. = Position
bwd = backward
fwd = forward
LOD = Line of direction
Contra = the opposite foot on the other side/dèan a-rithist air an taobh eile.

Line of direction (LOD) — The imaginary line running between your heels from back to front when standing in 1st Pos. flat. All directions stem from this imaginary line.

Obair nan Cas
THE FOOT POSITIONS

STARTING POSITION (applies only to Hebridean dancing.)
LF is in 1st Pos. (flat) and RF is placed in 3rd Pos. (flat).
When executing a **Bow,** step from the above mentioned position to 2nd Pos. (flat) on the RF; close in LF to 3rd Pos. (flat) — Bow — Step LF to 2nd Pos. (flat), back to starting position, close RF in to 3rd Pos. (flat).

The same applies to the **Finishing Bow or Curtsey / Dèan modh**; but step to the side, i.e., L or R, depending on what is most convenient as to which foot the weight is on at the last count of the dance.

FIRST INVERTED POSITION (1st Inverted Pos.)
A Closed Pos. — With weight equally distributed on both feet (flat), toes touching, they are turned in at an angle of 90 degrees or 45 degrees each from the line of direction.

INVERTED SECOND POSITION (Inverted 2nd Pos.)
An Open Pos. — Place the working foot in 2nd Pos. with toe touching the ground, heel is turned outwards and forwards, and knee turned inwards. The working leg is slightly bent.

SECOND FORWARD POSITION (2nd fwd Pos.)
An Open Pos. — The working foot is placed slightly forward of 2nd Pos. (A non-frequent position).

SECOND FORWARD AERIAL POSITION (2nd fwd Aer. Pos.)
An Open Aer. Pos. — As for 2nd fwd Pos. but pointed and lifted to the stated level. (A non-frequent position).

THIRD INVERTED POSITION (3rd Inverted Pos.)
A Closed Flat Pos. — Placed flat, toes pointing in and heels out, the toe of the working foot touches the instep of the supporting foot. Both feet are turned in at an angle of 45 degrees from the line of direction.

THIRD AERIAL POSITION (3rd Aer. Pos.)
A Closed Aer. Pos. — Working foot is held vertical and placed with the heel slightly below the knee, the whole of the outside of the working foot is in contact with the front of the supporting leg; the knee is well pressed back

towards 2nd Pos., to let the apron of the kilt remain flat. This is normal level.
3rd Aer. Pos. Low — the toe is in line with the ankle of the supporting leg.
3rd Aer. Pos. Very Low — the toe is slightly off the floor in 3rd Pos.

THIRD REAR AERIAL POSITION (3rd Rear Aer. Pos.)
A Closed Aer. Pos. — Same height as 3rd Aer. Pos. but the working foot is held vertical at the rear, with the inside edge touching the calf of the supporting leg. The foot should not be visible from the front. The knee of the working leg should be well pressed back.
3rd Rear Aer. Pos. Low — the toe is in line with the ankle of the supporting leg.
3rd Rear Aer. Pos. Very Low — the toe is slightly off the floor in 3rd Rear Pos.

FOURTH MIDWAY POSITION (4th Midway Pos.)
An Open Pos. — The working foot is pointed halfway between 4th Pos. and 4th Int. Pos. The position is used only for Shuffles. Position also known simply as ''Midway Pos.'

FOURTH MIDWAY AERIAL POSITION (4th Midway Aer. Pos.)
An Open Aer. Pos. — As for 4th Midway Pos. but pointed and lifted to a **Low** Aer. level. Used only for Shuffles.

Obair nan Làmh
HANDWORK

THE ARM POSITIONS:

1st Position — Place both hands on hips, the elbows are pointing directly to the side; the backs of the hands are facing the front, knuckles towards body and wrists are kept straight. Head faces straight forward with eyes level.

2nd Position — One hand is placed on the hip (1st Pos.) and the other is curved and lifted at the side, in line with the head, the palm of hand facing inwards. The hand is not raised as much as in Highland dancing. The head is facing diagonally away from the raised arm with chin slightly raised.

3rd Position — Both arms are lifted as for 2nd Pos. and more curved and not so high as in Highland dancing. Head faces straight forward.

4th Position — As for 3rd Pos. but hands held higher and closer (almost touching) — does not apply to Hebridean dancing.

5th Position — Both arms are gently curved in front of the body. Hands are held close, but do not touch the kilt. Does not apply to Hebridean dancing.

6th Position — One arm in Hebridean 2nd Pos. the other arm curved and hand held in front of the stomach (palm inwards).

Hands Clasped In Front — (Used in *Tulach Gorm*) — Arms curved in front of body; palm of left hand held straight and palm facing down; right hand is holding the left hand, thumb on top and other four fingers curved under palm of left hand.

Fingers Interlaced — Palms are held downwards, fingers are interlaced and no thumbs sticking out, arms are held fairly straight, or slightly, curved down in front of body.

Hands Clasped Behind Back — Both arms are held behind back and hands are clasped together, palms facing backwards.

Finger Grouping — The thumb sits at the side of the second finger beside the first joint. This differs from the Highland style of finger grouping where the end of the thumb sits under the second finger at the first joint.

Obair Cinn
HEADWORK

The head is facing forward along the line of direction, eyes level, when arms are in all positions except 2nd Pos.

When in 2nd Pos. the head faces away from the raised arm (diagonally right or left from the line of direction). The chin is slightly raised.

Gluasadnan Bunait
FOUNDATION MOVEMENTS:

Hop — the body weight is elevated and is begun on the ball of one foot and alights on the ball of the same foot.

Spring — the body weight is elevated and is begun on the ball of one foot and alights on the ball of the other foot.

Step — (with or without travel) a step is transfering weight from one foot to the ball or heel of the other foot. May be finished on a flat foot, if so stated.

Beat — as for step, but placing the ball or heel of the working foot is more accented and the movement involves no travelling.

Assemble —Begins with one foot in an aerial position, elevate and land on balls of both feet simultaneously in a specified closed position.
> FIOS / NOTE: Whenever assembling in 3rd Pos. or closing in to 3rd Rear Pos. do so with a good knee bend.

Disassemble — Begins with balls of both feet in a closed position, weight equally distributed on both feet, elevate and land on the ball of one foot with the other foot raised to, or placed in, a stated position.

Change — One foot is placed in 3rd or 5th Pos., demi-plié and elevate stretching toes towards the ground; and land with change of feet in same (3rd or 5th) Position.

Spread — From a closed position (i.e., 3rd or 5th Pos.) both legs are extended (sliding) towards 2nd Pos.; stand on balls of feet in 2nd Pos. with slightly bent knees before sliding back into 3rd or 5th position again. (Count: 'and').

Backstepping — Depending on the previous movement the Backstep may begin with the working foot (RF) in 3rd Aer. Pos., 3rd Rear Aer. Pos. or, sliding RF up in front of L leg to reach 3rd Aer. Pos. — Pass RF with a round-the-leg action to 3rd Rear Aer. Pos.; then slide RF down the back of L leg as you **spring on to it**, while sliding LF up the front of R to reach 3rd Aer. Pos. simultaneously on landing. Count '1'.
> Repeat contra, i.e., bring LF with a round-the-leg action to 3rd Rear Aer., slide down the back of R leg as you **spring on to it,** while bringing the RF up to 3rd Aer. Pos. Count '2'. One Backstep to each Count.

Ceum cùl dùbailte — (Hop-Backstep) — Hop LF, taking RF to 3rd Rear Aer. Pos. (and); Step RF in 3rd Rear Pos. (1); Hop RF, bring LF to 3rd Rear Aer. Pos. (and); Step LF in 3rd Rear Pos. (2). Repeat as required.

In *Till A-Rithist* the working foot already is in 3rd Rear Aer. Pos. when the movement begins which means a slight pause of action for the working foot at the beginning of each backstep sequence.

This movement is similar to 'Skips' forward or back in National Dancing. It is also known, by various sources, as either 'Hebridean Backsteps' or 'Shetland Backsteps'.

Bourrée — Is a movement of three small steps travelling sideways. The movement may be preceded with a small hop ('and'). There are four different Bourrées:

Bourrée Devant — (French 'before'); Step RF in 5th Pos., Step LF towards 2nd Pos. and Step RF in 5th Pos. (Front-Side-Front). Count: '1 and 2'.

Bourrée Derrière — (French 'behind'); Step RF in 5th Rear Pos., Step LF towards 2nd Pos., Step RF in 5th Rear Pos. (Behind-Side-Behind). Count: '1 and 2'.

Bourrée Under — Step RF in 5th Rear Pos., Step LF towards 2nd Pos., Step RF in 5th Pos. (Behind-Side-Front). Count: '1 and 2'.

Bourrée Over — Step RF in 5th Pos., Step LF towards 2nd Pos., Step RF in 5th Rear Pos. (Front-Side-Behind). Count: '1 and 2'.
> FIOS / NOTE 1: In **Hebridean Dancing** there is no extension prior to the Bourrée and knees are relaxed when closing feet to 5th (rear) positions. When travelling sideways the feet are gliding on the floor rather than stepping.

Toe-and-Heel — Hop or Spring, pointing the working foot in a specified position (i.e., 2nd, 3rd, 5th, or 4th-Opposite-5th-Pos), (1); Hop and place the working foot, well turned out (90 degrees from the LOD), on Heel in the same specified position (2). Repeat contra or as stated in the step description. Occupies two beats of music.

Heel-and-Toe — As for Toe-and-Heel movement but is used only in 3rd or 5th Pos. Two counts of music.

Heel - Toe - Beat — With RF — Beat R Heel in 2nd Pos. (1); Beat RF on ball in 2nd Pos. (and); Beat LF on ball in place (a). If a sideways movement occurs, the supporting foot (LF above) moves into 3rd Rear Pos. on the beat (a). Count '1 and a'. Repeat as required.

The beats with heel and ball should be strongly accented. (A Hebridean movement — applies only to *Till A-Rithist*).

Heel-and-Toe Travel — Travelling towards a specified position, usually 2nd or 4th Int. Pos.

With RF: Step RF on Heel in the specified position (and); Close LF to 3rd Rear Pos. on ball (1); Step RF on Toe (or Half-Point or Ball) to the specified position (and), Close LF to 5th Rear Pos. on Ball (2). Repeat as desired. Also done on LF.

FIOS / NOTE: The movement is done in series. May be preceded by a Hop, extending or taking the working foot to a specified position.

Toe-and-Heel Travel — As 'Heel-and-Toe Travel' but vice versa..

Seven-Step-Side Travel — Seven small steps taken high on the balls of feet travelling sideways and always away from the starting foot. May sometimes be preceded with a small Hop on the supporting foot ('and').

Travelling to the Left: Step RF in 5th Rear Pos. (1); Step LF towards 2nd Pos. (and); Step RF in 5th Rear Pos (2); Step LF towards 2nd Pos, Close RF to 5th Rear, Step LF to 2nd and Close RF to 5th Rear Pos. (and 3 and 4).

Also done on LF contra. Close feet firmly and make the movement smooth. The counting is even — (and) 1 and 2 and 3 and 4.

FIOS / NOTE 1: May finish with an extension to a specified position.

FIOS / NOTE 2: The movement may also be done in a 'Weaving fashion' taking the foot 'closing in' alternatively to 5th Rear Pos or 5th Pos. Thus: '5th Rear—2nd—5th—2nd—5th Rear—2nd—5th' or vice versa..

Rock — Rocks are usually danced in series of 2, 4, 6 up to 9.

With the RF: Spring on to RF on ball, pointing the LF in 3rd Rear Pos. (1); Spring on to LF on ball, pointing the RF in 3rd or 5th Pos. (2). Repeat as desired. May also be danced on the LF contra.

The rear foot is always pointed first, and when pointing the working foot it touches the ground lightly. Aim for plenty of elevation and ensure both feet touch the floor simultaneously.

Round-the-leg — Having the working foot in 3rd Rear Aer. Pos. passing it smoothly and closely round-the-supporting leg to 3rd Aer. Pos keeping the correct height throughout. The foot is in contact with the supporting leg all through the action. Also done vice versa, from front to back.

Shedding — Hop or Spring on to one foot, pointing the working foot to 2nd Pos. (without placing any weight on it (1); Hop, bringing the working foot sharply up to 3rd Rear Aer. Pos. (2); Hop, bringing the working foot with a round-the-leg action to 3rd Aer. Pos. (3); Hop, bringing the working foot with a round-the-leg action to 3rd Rear Aer. Pos. (4). Count: '1 2 3 4'.

Highland Fling Turn — To the Left: Hop LF, pointing RF in 2nd Pos. (1); On the next 3 counts make a complete turn to the Left on the spot (1/3 of a turn on each count): Hop LF, bringing RF to 3rd Rear Aer. Pos. (2); Hop LF, taking RF with a round-the-leg movement to 3rd Aer, Pos. (3); Hop LF, taking RF with a round-the-leg movement to 3rd Rear Aer. Pos. (4). Also done contra, turning to the Right.

High Cut — A movement done in series. Hop, Spring or Disassemble, bringing the working foot simultaneously on landing to 3rd Rear Aer. Pos.; extend the working foot towards 2nd Aer. Pos. and return it crisply to 3rd Rear Aer. Pos. (1 and); Spring on to the working foot repeat the movement contra (2 and). Maintain a good turnout of the knees. The movement of the High Cut comes from the knee joint.

Extensions of both feet towards 2nd position between the springs (and High Cut movements) does not apply to Hebridean Dancing. The counting is kept even.

High Cut In Front — Hop, Spring or Disassemble, extending the working foot to 4th Int. Aer. Pos., simultaneously on landing bring it in to 3rd Aer. Pos. (1); re-extend the working foot towards 4th Int. Aer. Pos. and return it with a crisp movement to 3rd Aer. Pos. (and). Make sure to use plenty of elevation on the hop. High Cut In Front is not danced in series.

Pas de Basque — With RF: Spring on to RF (1); place LF on Half-Point in 3rd or 5th Pos. (and); without exaggeration, beat the RF in 3rd or 5th Rear Pos on Ball, and if required, extend the LF simultaneously to a specified position to begin the next movement (2). The Pas de Basque may be preceded by an extension of the working foot (RF) to a Low Aer. Pos. (usually 2nd Aer. Pos. Low). In Hebridean dancing the counting is even '1 and 2, 3 and 4'.

Point-Close-Beat — With RF extended in 4th Int. Aer. Pos., hop LF and place RF on the half point in 4th Int. Pos. (no weight) (1); Close RF on the half point in to 5th (or 3rd) Pos. (and); Beat LF in 3rd Rear Pos., simultaneously lifting RF to a low 3rd Aer. Pos. (toes touching the left foot) (2). Count: ' 1 and 2'.

Shake — Almost always preceded with a Hop, pointing the working foot in 5th Pos. (1); the shake is performed in conjunction with the next Hop; extend the working foot to 4th Int. Aer. Pos. Low (and); bring it back slightly before extending it fully with a pointed foot to 4th Int. Aer. Pos. (a 2). When the working foot reaches the 4th Int. Aer. Pos. it does so upon landing from the accompanying Hop. Count: '(1) and a 2'. May also be executed towards 2nd Aer. Pos. and 2nd Forward Aer. Pos.

Shake — (For *Caisteal Chiosamul* only): From 5th Pos. RF is extended to 4th Int. Aer. Pos. (and); brought back a little before being extended fully to a High 4th Int. Aer. Pos. (a). The landing of the hop LF in this movement occurs simultaneously as RF reaches it highest point on count 'a'. The Shakes should be strongly accented without being stiff in the movement. Count 'and a'.

Shuffles — Spring onto one foot and place the other one on ball in 4th Midway Pos. and brush it in to 3rd Pos. (1); Brush it out to 4th Midway Pos. (and). The foot never leaves the floor. Supporting leg should be slightly bent. Repeat Contra. (Arms: 1st Pos.) (Applies only to Hebridean dancing).

Double Shuffles — Spring on to one foot and place the other one on ball in 4th Midway Pos. and brush it in to 3rd Pos. and Brush it out to 4th Midway Pos. (1). Repeat — Brush in and out again (and).
   The foot never leaves the floor. Supporting leg should be slightly bent. Repeat Contra. (Arms: 1st Pos.) (Applies only to Hebridean dancing).

Treble Shuffles — Spring on to one foot and place the other one on ball in 4th Midway Pos. and quickly brush it in to 3rd Pos. (1); out again halfway to 4th Midway Pos. (and); brush it in to 3rd Pos. (and); brush it out to 4th Midway Pos. (a).
   The foot never leaves the ground and the movement is very quick. Spring on to the working foot and repeat the movement Contra. (Arms: 1st Pos.)
Count:5 and and a, 6 and and a, 7 and and a, 8 and and a.
(Applies only to Hebridean dancing).
Pivot Turn — **Turning to the Left**: Place the RF in 3rd Crossed Pos. on Half-Point close to the LF, while starting to pivot to the left on ball of LF. Pivot all the way round to the left high on balls of both feet, **without displacing** them, finishing with LF in front in 3rd or 5th Pos. Count: '7 8'.
Turning to the Right: As above but contra.

FIOS / NOTE 1: The movement may be preceded by an extension of the working foot to 4th Int. Aer. Pos.

FIOS / NOTE 2: The higher upon balls of feet and the quicker the movement is executed the easier it become. Keep weight equally distributed on both feet.

Shake-Shake-Down — Hop, making a shake action with the working foot in 4th Int.Aer. Pos. (1); Bringing the working foot slightly inwards, Hop, making another shake action with the same foot to 2nd Aer. Pos. (and); Spring on to the working foot in 5th Rear Pos. and if required, simultaneously extend the supporting foot to an open aerial position to begin the next movement. (2).

FIOS / NOTE: Both shake actions may be done to 2nd Aer. Pos.

Skip Change of Step — With RF. Hop LF, extending RF to 4th Aer. Pos. Low (and); Step RF towards 4th Pos. on ball (1); Close LF to 3rd Rear Pos. (feet touching) (and); Step RF towards 4th Pos. on ball (2). Repeat contra, bringing the LF through 1st Pos. to 4th Aer. Pos. Low on the first Hop (and).
Count: 'and 1 and 2, and 3 and 4'.

FIOS / NOTE: In some of the Hebridean Dances, the Skip Change may be more of a gliding forward. See *Bonaidean Gorma* and *Scotch Measure*.

Treble — (Used in *Caisteal Chiosamul*) — With RF: Shuffle (Beat) RF out towards 4th Int. Aer. Pos. Low (and); Shuffle (Beat) RF inwards to 3rd Aer. Pos. Low off leg (and); Beat RF in 3rd Pos. on Ball (a); Beat LF in 3rd Rear Pos. on Ball (1). Same with LF but danced contra.

Make the beats distinctive. Do not confuse this movement with Trebles in National dances or Shuffling in the *Sailors' Hornpipe*.

——o0o——

Tulach Gorm
(A Solo Dance)

An Ceòl: Strathspey *Tulloch Gorm.*
Tempo: 40 Bars per minute.   Crotchet = 116 per minute.
Time: 4/4, 4 Bar Introduction   8 Bars to each step.
Count: 4 Counts to each Bar.

Tha *Tulach Gorm* a' sealltainn na tulaich air am biodh fear faire a' seasamh a' cumail sùil a-mach airson nàimhdean a' Phrionnsa Teàrlaich.
Tha e air a dhannsa air an spot gun ghluasad gu taobh seach taobh air eagal amharas a thoirt seachad. Tha mòran dol mun cuairt ann cuideachd airson gum b' urrainn dha sùil shèolta a chumail air a h-uile taobh.

Tulach Gorm is the only Hebridean dance that has been known by its Gaelic name only since it was devised. The Gaelic translates to *The Green Knoll* and in local myth the movements of the dance is supposed to relate to the knolls or mounds the lookouts stood on, watching out for the enemies of Bonnie Prince Charlie. Not to look suspicious they performed this dance, it is said, and all the steps are performed more or less on the spot with turns to get a good view of the surroundings. The sharp head movements are also supposed to indicate the watchman's surveillance of the neighbourhood.[1] Farquar MacNeil states that the Green Knoll was where Prince Charlie and Flora parted.

In truth, the dance is another 'Highland Fling' arrangement. It is sometimes said to be the forerunner of the Highland Fling, but most likely they existed side by side, as the 'Fling', is really only an assembled number of different Reel steps.

[1] This story is from Katie Ann Mackinnon

Na Comharraichean — NOTES

An Ceòl/ Music — The dance was written to and is best performed to the Strathspey 'Tulloch Gorm'
(6 steps covering 48 bars).

Obair cinn/Headwork — The head should be turned sharply from side to side or to face front in co-ordination with the arm movements.

Obair nan Làmh / Handwork — The armwork for this dance follows the same pattern as for other solo Hebridean dances. i.e The opposite arm to the working foot is raised in 2nd Pos. During Shuffles, both arms are in 1st Pos. A special hand grip is explained in the 5th Step / An còigeamh ceum.

6th Position — **L:** Left arm in Hebridean 2nd Pos. R arm curved and hand held in front of the stomach (palm inwards). **R:** Repeat contra.

This dance should be danced very crisply, with sharp extensions to all Open Aerial Positions.

Gluasadan sònraichte — SPECIAL MOVEMENTS
Ball of foot is used unless otherwise stated.

Shuffles — Single, Double or Treble Shuffles as to the dancers capability, but must be consistent throughout the dance. Treble Shuffles apply only for Men dancing the *Tulach Gorm*.

Tòiseachadh — INTRODUCTION
Bars

1 - 2   Stand with Head, Arms and Feet in Hebridean starting position.
Count: 1 2 3 4, 5 6 7 8.

3 - 4   Step to the right, closing LF in front and make a slow and deep Bow - Count: 1 2 3 4, 5 6 7 8
Rise on balls of feet on Count 8.

A' chiad cheum — FIRST STEP
'Side, Behind, Cut, Cut'
Bars

1   With a disassemble on to LF point RF in 2nd Pos. (1);
Hop on LF bringing RF to 3rd Rear Aer. Pos. (2);
Hop on LF extending RF halfway to 4th Int. Aer. Pos. (and);
Bring RF to 3rd Aer. Pos. (3);
Hop on LF extending RF halfway to 4th Int. Aer. Pos. (and);
Bring RF to 3rd Aer. Pos. (4).

FIOS / NOTE: When extending RF for the cuts in 3rd Aer., the working leg should hang vertically on its outmost point. It is a short and crisp movement.

Count: 1 2 and 3 and4

2   With a Spring RF, repeat Bar 1 contra.

Count: 5 6 and 7 and8

3   With a Spring LF, repeat Bar 1.

Count: 1 2 and 3 and 4

4   Spring onto RF dance 4 Treble Shuffles (Springing R.L.R.L.) or ordinary Shuffles.

Count: 5 and and a, 6 and and a, 7 and and a, 8 and and a

(5 and 6 and 7 and 8 and)

Obair nan Làmh / Handwork — 2nd Pos. in opposition on Bars

1 - 3   1st Pos. on Bar 4

5 - 8   With a Spring RF, repeat Bars 1 - 4 contra.

An dara ceum — SECOND STEP
'Front, Behind'

Bars

1   With a Spring LF bring RF to 3rd Aer. Pos (1);
        Hop on LF taking RF to 3rd Rear Aer. Pos. (2);
        Assemble with bent knees RF in 5th Pos. (3);
        Step (glide) to 2nd Pos. on RF (and);
        Close LF to 5th Rear Pos., finish with knees bent (4).
        Hold counts as long as possible!
        Count: 1 2 3 and 4

Obair nan Làmh / Handwork — 6th Pos. L .

2   With a Spring RF, repeat Bar 1 contra.
        Count: 5 6 7 and 8

3   With a Spring LF, repeat Bar 1.
        Count: 1 2 3 and 4

4   Spring on to RF dance 4 Treble Shuffles.
        (Springing R.L.R.L.) or ordinary Shuffles.
        Count: 5 and and a, 6 and and a, 7 and and a, 8 and and a
        (5 and 6 and 7 and 8 and).
        Obair nan Làmh / Handwork — 1st Pos.

5 - 8   With a Spring RF, repeat Bars 1 - 4 contra.

                    An treas ceum — THIRD STEP
                    'Side in front and Turn'
Bars
1   With a Spring LF, point RF in 2nd Pos. (1);
        Hop on LF bringing RF to 3rd Aer. Pos. (2);
        Springing on to RF point LF in 2nd Pos. (3);
        Hop on RF bringing LF to 3rd Aer. Pos. (4).
        Count: 1 2 3 4
        Obair nan Làmh / Handwork — 2nd Pos. in opposition.

2   With a Spring LF point RF in 2nd Pos. (5);
        Making a full turn to the Left, Hop LF bringing RF to 3rd
        Rear Aer. Pos. (6);
        Facing the front, Hop LF pointing RF in 2nd Pos. (7);
        Hop LF bringing RF to 3rd Aer. Pos. (8).
        Count: 5 6 7 8
        Obair nan Làmh / Handwork — 1st Pos. on counts '5 6' 2nd
        Pos. L on counts '7 8'

3   With a Spring RF, repeat Bar 1 contra.
        Count: 1 2 3 4

4   With a Spring RF, repeat Bar 2 contra.
        Count: 5 6 7 8

5 - 8   With a Hop RF, repeat Bars 1 - 4 contra.

An ceathramh ceum — FOURTH STEP
'Toe, Heel'

Bars

1   With a Hop on LF point RF in 5th Pos. (1);
Hop on LF, place RF on Heel in 5th Pos. (2),
Spring on to RF point LF in 5th Pos. (3);
Hop on RF, place LF on Heel in 5th Pos. (4).
Count: 1 2 3 4

Obair nan Làmh / Handwork — 3rd Pos.

2   With a Spring LF dance 4 Treble Shuffles (Springing
L.R.L.R.) or ordinary Shuffles.
Count: 5 and and a, 6 and and a, 7 and and a, 8 and and a
(5 and 6 and 7 and 8 and)

Obair nan Làmh / Handwork — 1st Pos.

3 - 4   With a Hop RF, repeat Bars 1 - 2 contra.
Count: 1 2 3 4, 5 and and a, 6 and and a, 7 and and a,
8 and and a (5 and 6 and 7 and 8 and)

5 - 8   With a Hop LF, repeat Bars 1-4.

An còigeamh ceum — FIFTH STEP
'Rocks, Cuts and Shake'

Bars

1   With a Spring onto RF execute 4 Rocks in 5th Pos.
(Springing R.L.R.L.).
Count: 1 2 3 4

Obair nan Làmh / Handwork — Hands clasped together in 5th
Pos. with arms slightly bent.
Palms together; L palm is facing down and held by R hand,
with R thumb on top of L hand.

2   With a Spring RF, bring LF from slightly towards 4th Int.
Rear Aer. Pos. into 3rd Rear Aer. Pos. simultaneously on
landing (L knee is bent) (5);
Hop RF, re-extend LF slightly towards 4th Int. Rear Aer.
Pos. and bring it back again to 3rd Rear Aer. Pos.
simultaneously on landing (L knee bent)(6);
Hop RF, pointing LF in 5th Pos. (7);

33

Hop RF, extending LF with a Shake to 4th Int. Aer. Pos. (and 8).In this movement the knee is held fairly still, with only the lower leg and foot working, the leg is bent at the knee-joint and well turned out.

Count: 5 6 7 and 8

Obair nan Làmh / Handwork — 2nd Pos. R

3 - 4　　With a Spring LF, repeat Bars 1 - 2 contra.

Count: 1 2 3 4, 5 6 7 and 8

5 - 8　　With a Spring RF to begin, repeat Bars 1 - 4.

An t-siathamh ceum — SIXTH STEP
'Turning'

Bars

1　　Hopping on LF, dance Bar 1 of FIRST STEP but a **complete turn** to the Left is made on Count **'2'**, to face front on Counts 'and 3 and 4.'

Count: 1 2 and 3 and 4

Obair nan Làmh / Handwork —2nd Pos. L

2　　With a Spring RF, repeat Bar 1 contra, turning to the Right.

Count: 5 6 and 7 and 8

3　　With a Spring LF, repeat Bar 1.

Count: 1 2 and 3 and 4

4　　Spring RF, dance 4 Treble Shuffles (Springing R.L.R.L.) or ordinary Shuffles.

Count: 5 and and a, 6 and and a, 7 and and a, 8 and and a
(5 and 6 and 7 and 8 and).

Obair nan Làmh / Handwork — 1st Pos.

5 - 8　　With a Spring RF, repeat bars 1 - 4 contra.

A' Chrìoch — FINISH

Step to 2nd Pos. on LF, Close RF to LF in Hebridean Starting Pos. (flat) and Bow or Curtsey — Dèan modh.

Thairis An Aiseig Gu Teàrlach
(Over the Waters)
(A Solo Dance)

An Ceòl: *Over the Water to Charlie.*
Tempo: 52 - 54 Bars per minute is the ideal speed.
         Crotchet = 104 - 108.
Time: 6/8, 8-Bar Introduction.   16 Bars to each step.
Count: 2 Counts to each Bar.

Dannsa aon-neach air a dhannsa le port dannsa cruinn (jig). Tha e a' sealltainn mar a chaidh na h-Eileanaich tarsainn an Aiseig a chuideachadh a' Phrionnsa Teàrlaich aig àm Ar-a-mach nan Seumasach. Chithear sin gu follaiseach anns an treas ceum a' 'Siubhal' bho Eilean gu Eilean.

Over the Water to Charlie sometimes known as *Over the Water*, or *Over the Waters*. This solo Jig is known in several versions, and the prominent feature are the many 'Point-close-beat' movements. This suggests that these steps might have evolved, or borrowed the style, from the older styles of dancing.

    In the local Island myth this dance has a story attached to it according to Katie Ann Mackinnon, the story goes that the dance shows how the island clansmen travelled 'over the waters' to the mainland to fight for Bonnie Prince Charlie in the '45 Jacobite Rebellion. The third step is supposed to clearly show the hopping from island to island to reach the Prince on the mainland.

Na Comharraichean — NOTES

An Ceòl / Music — This dance is preferably performed to the Jig *Over the Water to Charlie* (6 steps covering 96 bars).

Obair nan Làmh / Handwork — The armwork for this dance follows the same pattern as for Scottish Solo Highland dances. i.e: The opposite arm to the working foot is raised in 2nd Pos. During Aer. Spring Point movements and Changes, both arms are in 1st Pos.

Gluasadan sònraichte — SPECIAL MOVEMENTS

Ball of foot is used unless otherwise stated.
5th Pos. should be used consistently throughout the dance.

Point-Close-Beat
Shuffles — Single, Double or Treble Shuffles as to the dancers capability, but whatever choice must be used consistently throughout the dance.

Tòiseachadh — INTRODUCTION

Bars
1 - 4   Stand in Hebridean Starting Pos. (RF in front) with Arms at the sides. Count: 1 2, 3 4, 5 6, 7 8.

5 - 6   Step to the right, closing LF in front — Bow or Curtsey — Count: 1 2, 3 4

7 - 8   Step back to stand in Hebridean Starting Pos. (RF in front) — Count: 5 6, 7 8

A' chiad cheum — FIRST STEP
'Side, behind, Point-Close-Beat'

Bars
1 - 2   With a disassemble on to LF, point RF in 2nd Pos. (1);
Hop LF, bring RF to 3rd Rear Aer. Pos. (2);
Dance a Point-Close-Beat movement with RF (3 and4).
Count: 1 2, 3 and 4

3 - 4   With a Spring RF, repeat Bars 1 - 2 contra.
Count: 5 6, 7 and 8

5 - 6   With a Spring LF, repeat Bars 1 - 2.
Count: 1 2, 3 and4

7 - 8   Extend RF to 4th Int. Aer. Pos. as preparation for the spring:
Spring RF, LF, RF, LF, execute 4 Treble Shuffles
(or ordinary Shuffles).

36

Count: 5 and and a 6 and and a, 7 and and a 8 and and a
[5 and 6 and 7 and 8 and].
Obair nan Làmh / Handwork — 2nd Pos. in opposition on Bars
1 - 6.
1st Pos. on Bars 7-8.

9 - 16   With a Spring RF, repeat Bars 1 - 8 contra.

An dara ceum — SECOND STEP
'Inverted Toe and Heel'

Bars

1 - 2   With a spring LF, place RF on toe to the side in 2nd Inverted
Pos. with knees touching (1);
Hop LF, place RF on Heel in 2nd Pos. (2);
Hop LF, taking RF to 3rd Rear Aer. Pos. (3);
Hop LF, holding RF in 3rd Rear Aer. Pos. (and);
Spring RF, taking LF to 3rd Low Aer. Pos. (4).
On counts '3 and 4' there is a sideways movement to the left
towards 2nd Pos.
Count: 1 2, 3 and 4
Obair nan Làmh / Handwork —2nd Pos. L on counts '1 2'.
3rd Pos. on counts '3 and 4'

3 - 4   With a Hop RF, repeat Bars 1 - 2 contra, travelling to
the right.
Count: 5 6, 7 and 8

5 - 6   With a Hop LF, repeat Bars 1 - 2, travelling to the left.
Count: 1 2, 3 and 4

7 - 8   Spring LF, RF, LF, RF execute 4 Treble Shuffles
(or ordinary Shuffles).
Count: 5 and and a 6 and and a, 7 and and a, 8 and and a
[5 and 6 and 7 and 8 and].
Obair nan Làmh / Handwork —1st Pos.

9 - 16   With a Hop RF, repeat Bars 1 - 8 contra.

An treas ceum — THIRD STEP
'Over the Water step'

Bars

1 - 2   With a Hop LF, dance Point-Close-Beat with RF (1 and 2);
Travelling straight forward, Extend RF and Spring RF
towards 4th Pos., simultaneously on landing taking LF to 3rd
Rear Aer. Pos. (Hold position as long as possible) (3);
Extend LF andSpring LF towards 4th Pos., simultaneously on
landing taking RF to 3rd Rear Aer. Pos. (4).
Count: 1 and2, 3 4

   Obair nan Làmh / Handwork — 2nd Pos. L on Bar 1, 3rd Pos.
   on Bar 2

3 - 4   Extending RF towards 4th Int. Aer. Pos. to prepare, Hop LF,
execute a Point-Close-Beat movement with RF (5 and 6);
Travelling backwards to starting position: Hop LF twice
Taking RF to 3rd Aer. Pos., passing it round-the-leg to 3rd
Rear Aer. Pos. during the two hops. (7 and);
Spring RF, taking LF to 3rd Aer. Pos. Low (8).
Count: 5 and 6, 7 and 8

   Obair nan Làmh / Handwork — 2nd Pos. L on Bar 3
   3rd Pos. on Bar 4

5 - 8   With a Hop RF, repeat Bars 1- 4 contra.
Count: 1 and 2, 3 4, 5 and 6, 7 and 8

9 - 16   With a Hop LF, repeat Bars 1 - 8.

An ceathramh ceum — FOURTH STEP
'Point-Close-Beat and Assemble-Step-Close'

Bars

1 - 2   With a Hop LF, execute a Point-Close-Beat movement with RF (1 and 2);
Spring RF, execute a Point-Close-Beat movement with LF (3 and 4).
Count: 1 and 2, 3 and 4
Obair nan Làmh / Handwork — 2nd Pos. in opposition

3 - 4   Assemble RF in 5th Pos. (bent knees) (5);
Step (glide) RF towards 2nd Pos. (and);
Close LF to 5th Rear Pos. (with bent knees) (6);
Assemble LF in 5th Pos. (bent knees) (7);
Step (glide) LF towards 2nd Pos. (and);
Close RF in 5th Rear Pos. (with bent knees) (8).
FIOS / NOTE: There are no extensions prior to the assembles.
Count: 5 and 6, 7 and 8
Obair nan Làmh / Handwork — 3rd Pos.

5 - 6   With a disassemble onto LF, repeat Bars 1 - 2.
Count: 1 and 2, 3 and 4

7 - 8   Extend LF to 4th Int. Aer. Pos. as preparation for the spring:
Spring LF, RF, LF, RF, execute 4 Treble
Shuffles (or ordinary Shuffles).
Count: 5 and and a 6 and and a, 7 and and a 8 and and a
[5 and 6 and 7 and 8 and].
Obair nan Làmh / Handwork — 1st Pos.

9 - 16   With a Hop RF, repeat Bars 1 - 8 contra.

An còigeamh ceum — FIFTH STEP
'Front, behind and Turn'

Bars

1 - 2   With a Hop LF, execute a Point-Close-Beat movement with RF (1 and2);
Hop LF, bringing RF to 3rd Aer.Pos. (3);
Hop LF, bringing RF with a round-the-leg movement to 3rd Rear Aer. Pos. (4).
Count: 1 and 2, 3 4

Obair nan Làmh / Handwork — 2nd Pos. L.

3 - 4   Hop LF, executing a Point-Close-Beat movement with RF (5 and 6);
Making a complete turn to the right on the spot on counts 7 and 8': Hop LF, bringing RF to 3rd Aer. Pos. (7);
Hop LF bring RF with a round-the-leg action to 3rd Rear Aer. Pos. (and);
Spring RF, taking LF to 3rd Aer. Pos. Low (8).
Count: 5 and 6, 7 and 8

Obair nan Làmh / Handwork — 2nd Pos. L on Bar 3.
3rd Pos. on Bar 4.

5 - 8   With a Hop RF, repeat Bars 1 - 4 contra.
Count: 1 and 2, 3 4, 5 and 6, 7 and 8

9 - 16   With a Hop LF, repeat Bars 1 - 8.

An t-siathamh ceum — SIXTH STEP
'Point-Close-Beat'

Bars

1 - 2   Hopping on LF, execute Point-Close-Beat movement twice
           with RF.
           Count: 1 and 2, 3 and 4

3 - 4   Spring then Hop RF, execute Point-Close-Beat movement
           twice with LF.
           Count: 5 and 6, 7 and 8

5 - 6   Spring LF, execute a Point-Close Beat movement with RF
           (1 and 2);
           Spring RF, execute a Point-Close-Beat movement with LF
           (3 and4).
           Count: 1 and 2, 3 and 4

7 - 8   Spring LF, RF, LF, RF, execute 4 Treble Shuffles
           (or ordinary Shuffles).
           Count: 5 and and a 6 and and a, 7 and and a 8 and and a
           [5 and 6 and 7 and 8 and].
   Obair nan Làmh / Handwork — 2nd Pos. in opposition for Point-
           Close-Beat movements. 1st Pos. for Shuffles.

9 - 16   With a Hop RF, repeat Bars 1 - 8 contra.

A' Chrìoch — FINISH
Step to 2nd Pos. on RF, Close LF to RF in Hebridean Starting Pos. (flat)
and Bow or Curtsey — Dèan modh.

41

Mac Iain Ghasda
(A Solo Dance)

An Ceòl: *Mac Iain Ghasda / Highland Laddie.*
Tempo: 56 - 60 Bars per minute.
Time: 2/4, 8-Bar Introduction.   16 Bars to each step.
Count: 2 Counts to each Bar.

A rèir choltais chaidh an dannsa seo a shamlachadh air fonn a' phuirt *Mac Iain Ghasda.*

This seems to be a very common Highland step-dance, known in a number versions from various locations in Scotland. It is most often regarded as a man's dance, but a woman's version is known. Ewen MacLachlan is often credited for having composed the *Highland Laddie*, but the dance existed on the mainland prior to him starting out as a dance teacher, so he more likely had his own version to teach. This dance was always performed to the tune *Mac Iain Ghasda* (Son of Noble John), which is the Gaelic equivalent of the song *Highland Laddie*. The present day version of 'Highland Laddie' danced on the Isle of Barra and on South Uist is styled *Mac Iain Ghasda* by Sgoil Dannsa nan Eileanach.

Presented here are 6 steps plus an alternative step, which is just a variation of the fourth step. Only one of the two should be chosen when performing the dance.

Na Comharraichean — NOTES

Obair nan Làmh / Handwork — The man will follow the directions given below. When danced by a girl, she can either use the arm movements as stated or the skirt should be held lightly between thumb and forefinger of each hand throughout the dance.

Do not stilt movements in this dance. All movements should be natural and relaxed.

Gluasadan sònraichte — SPECIAL MOVEMENTS

Ball of foot is used unless otherwise stated.

Assemble - Whenever assembling in 5th Pos. or closing in to 5th Rear Pos. do so with a good knee bend.

Shake-Shake-Down — With RF — Hop on LF, extending RF with a Shake action to **2nd** Aer. Pos. (1); Hop LF, bringing RF in then re-extending it with a Shake action to 2nd Aer. Pos. (and); Spring both feet together with RF in 5th Rear Pos. raising LF to a very low 3rd Aer. Pos. (2).

For LF, dance above contra.

Ceum cùl dùbailte

Point-Close-Beat

Shuffles — Single, Double or Treble Shuffles as to the dancers capability, but must be used consistently throughout the dance.

Tòiseachadh — INTODUCTION

Bars

1 - 4   Stand in Hebridean Starting Pos. (RF in front) with Arms at the sides.
Count: 1 2, 3 4, 5 6, 7 8.

5 - 6   Step to the right, closing LF in front — Bow or Curtsey — Dèan modh — Count: 1 2, 3 4.

7 - 8   Step back to stand in Hebridean Starting Pos. (RF in front) — Count: 5 6, 7 8.

A' chiad cheum — FIRST STEP

Bars

1 - 2   With a disassemble on to LF, point RF in 2nd Pos. (1);
(make a complete turn on the spot to the Left on the next two counts), Hop LF, bringing RF to 3rd Rear Aer. Pos. (2);
Assemble RF in 5th Pos. (3);
Step RF to 2nd Pos. (and);
Close LF to 5th Rear Pos. (4).
Count: 1 2, 3 and 4
Obair nan Làmh / Handwork — 2nd Pos. L on Bar 1.
3rd Pos. on Bar 2.

3 - 4   Change LF to 5th Pos. (5);
Step to 2nd Pos. on LF (and);
Close RF to 5th Rear Pos. (6);
Change RF in 5th Pos. (7);
Step to 2nd Pos. on RF (and);
Close LF to 5th Rear Pos. (8).
Count: 5 and 6, 7 and 8
Obair nan Làmh / Handwork — 3rd Position.

5 - 6   With a disassemble on to RF, repeat Bars 1 - 2 contra.
Count: 1 2, 3 and 4

7 - 8   With a disassemble on to LF dance 4 Shuffles — Single,
Double, or Treble
(Springing L.R.L.R.)
Count: 5 and and a, 6 and and a, 7 and and a, 8 and and a
(counting for Treble Shuffles.)
Obair nan Làmh / Handwork — 1st Position.

9 - 16   With a Hop RF, repeat Bars 1 - 8 contra.

An dara ceum — SECOND STEP

Bars

1 - 2   Assemble with RF in 5th Pos. (1); Step RF to 2nd Pos. (and);
Close LF to 5th Rear Pos. (2);
Change LF to 5th Pos. (3); Step LF to 2nd Pos (and);
Close RF to 5th Rear Pos. (4).
Count: 1 and 2, 3 and 4
Obair nan Làmh / Handwork — 3rd Pos.

3 - 4   Disassemble onto RF executing a Shake-Shake-Down action
with LF (5 and 6);
Hop LF to begin, executing a Shake-Shake-Down action with
RF (7 and 8).
Count: 5 and 6, 7 and 8

5 - 6   With a Spring LF, execute a Point-Close-Beat movement with
RF (1 and 2);

44

Spring RF, execute a Point-Close-Beat movement with LF
(3 and 4).
Count: 1 and 2, 3 and 4
Obair nan Làmh / Handwork — 2nd Pos. in opposition.

7 - 8   With a Spring on to LF dance 4 Shuffles — Single, Double,
or Treble (Springing L.R.L.R.)
Count: 5 and and a, 6 and and a, 7 and and a, 8 and and a
(counting for Treble Shuffles)
Obair nan Làmh / Handwork — 1st Position.

9 - 16   With an Assemble LF in 5th Pos., repeat Bars 1 - 8 contra.

An treas ceum — THIRD STEP

Bars

1 - 2   Hop LF, dance a Point-Close-Beat movement with RF,
springing on to RF repeat with LF.
Count: 1 and 2, 3 and 4

3 - 4   Travelling towards R.D.F.: Spring on to LF, taking RF to 3rd
Rear Aer. Pos. (5);
Spring on to RF, taking LF to 3rd Rear Aer. Pos. (6).
FIOS / NOTE: The 2 springs are executed towards 4th Pos.
Travelling Backwards L.D.B. to starting position: Hop on RF with
LF in 3rd Rear Aer. Pos. (7); Hop on RF with LF in 3rd Rear Aer.
Pos. (and); Spring LF, taking RF to 3rd Low Aer. Pos. (8).
Count: 5 6, 7 and 8

5 - 6   With a Hop LF, repeat Bars 1 - 2.
Count: 1 and 2, 3 and 4

7 - 8   With a Spring on to LF dance 4 Shuffles — Single, Double,
or Treble (Springing L.R.L.R.)
Count: 5 and and a, 6 and and a, 7 and and a, 8 and and a
(counting for Treble Shuffles)

Obair nan Làmh / Handwork — 2nd Pos. in opposition on
Bars 1 - 2 and 5 - 6. 3rd Pos. on Bars 3 - 4.
1st Pos. on Bars 7 - 8.

9 - 16   With a Hop on RF, repeat Bars 1 - 8 contra.

An ceathramh ceum — FOURTH STEP

Bars
1 - 2   With a Hop LF (1);
Step towards 2nd Pos. on Heel of RF (and);
Close LF to 3rd Rear Pos. (2);
Step towards 2nd Pos. on Ball of RF (and);
Close LF to 5th Rear Pos. (3);
Step towards 2nd Pos. on Heel of RF (and);
Close LF to 3rd Rear Pos. (4);

Point RF to forward 2nd Pos. (and).
Count: 1 and 2, and 3 and 4 and

3 - 4   Placing the ball of RF in 3rd crossed Pos. (5);
Step towards 2nd Pos. on Heel of LF (and);
Close RF to 3rd Rear Pos. (6);
Step towards 2nd Pos. on Ball of LF (and);
Close RF to 5th Rear Pos. (7);
Step towards 2nd Pos. on Heel of LF (and);
Close RF to 3rd Rear Pos. (8);
Point LF to forward 2nd Pos. (and).
Count: 5 and 6, and 7 and 8 and

5 - 6   Disassemble on to LF, dance Point-Close-Beat Movement
with RF, springing RF repeat with LF.
Count: 1 and2, 3 and4
Obair nan Làmh / Handwork — 2nd Pos. in opposition on
Bars 1 - 6.

7 - 8   With a Spring on to LF dance 4 Shuffles — Single, Double,
or Treble (Springing L.R.L.R.)
Count: 5 and and a, 6 and and a, 7 and and a, 8 and and a
(counting for Treble Shuffles)
Obair nan Làmh / Handwork — 1st Position.

9 - 16   With a Hop RF, repeat Bars 1 - 8 contra.

An còigeamh ceum — FIFTH STEP

Bars

1 - 2   Hop LF, execute a Point-Close-Beat movement with RF
(1 and2);
Hop on LF simultaneously
Heel tap RF in 5th Pos. (3);
Heel tap RF in 5th Pos. leaving heel on the ground (and);
Beat LF (without exaggeration) in 5th Rear Pos. (4).
Count: 1 and 2, 3 and 4
Obair nan Làmh / Handwork — 2nd Pos. L.

47

3 - 4   Hop on LF, extending RF with a Shake action to 4th Int. Aer.
         Pos. (5);
         Hop LF, with a slight relaxation of the knee of R leg before,
         executing another Shake action to 4th Int. Aer. Pos. (and);
         Spring RF in 5th Rear Pos. (6);
         Step LF on heel towards 4th Int. Pos. (and);
         Close RF in 3rd Rear Pos. (7);
         Step LF on toe towards 4th Int. Pos. (and);
         Close RF to 5th Rear Pos. (8).
         Count: 5 and 6, and 7 and 8
   Obair nan Làmh / Handwork — 2nd Pos. in opposition, changing
   on count '6.'

5 - 8   With a disassemble on to RF, repeat Bars 1 - 4 contra.
         Count: 1 and 2, 3 and 4, 5 and 6, and 7 and 8

9 - 16   With a disassemble on to LF, repeat Bars 1 - 8.
         FIOS / NOTE: The sideways travel in this step may as an option be
         done towards 2nd Pos.

                    An t-siathamh ceum — SIXTH STEP
                         "Ceum cùl dùbailte"
Bars
1 - 2   With a disassemble on to LF, extend RF to 4th Int. Aer. Pos.
         (and); Bring RF immediately in to
         3rd Aer. Pos. executing a High Cut In Front (1and); Hop LF ,
         bringing RF to 3rd Rear Aer. Pos.,
         dance 3 Ceum cùl dùbailte stepping on to RF, LF, RF (a 2 and
         3 and 4).
         Count: and 1and a 2, and 3 and 4

3 - 4   With a Hop RF, repeat Bars 1 - 2 Contra.
         Count: and 5 and a 6, and 7 and 8

5 - 6   Hop LF, execute Point-Close-Beat movement with RF,
         Springing RF, Point-Close-Beat with LF.
         Count: 1 and 2, 3 and 4

48

Obair nan Làmh / Handwork: 2nd Pos. in opposition.
                                  3rd Pos. for Ceum cùl dùbailte.

7 - 8   With a Spring on to LF dance 4 Shuffles — Single, Double,
         or Treble (Springing L.R.L.R.)
         Count: 5 and and a, 6 and and a, 7 and and a, 8 and and a
         (counting for Treble Shuffles)
Obair nan Làmh / Handwork: 1st Position.

9 - 16   With a Hop RF, repeat Bars 1 - 8 contra.

Ceum air-leth — ALTERNATIVE STEP
Bars
1 - 16   Same as **An ceathramh ceum / Fourth Step**, but moving
         diagonally forward towards 4th Int. Pos. instead of towards
         2nd Pos. on the sideways travel on Bars 1 - 4 and 9 - 12.

A' Chrìoch — FINISH
Step to 2nd Pos. on RF, Close LF to RF in Hebridean Starting Pos. (flat)
and Bow or Curtsey — Dèan modh.

Bonaidean Gorma
Blue Bonnets
(A Solo Dance)

An Ceòl: *The Scots Blue Bonnets.*
Tempo: 56 - 60 Bars per minute.
Time: 6/8, 8-Bar Introduction.   16 Bars to each step.
Count: 2 Counts to each Bar.

'S e *Bonaidean Gorma* am prìomh dhannsa a chaidh a sheatadh ris a' phort *Scots Blue Bonnets*. Anns an leabhar seo chì sibh an dòigh san do dhanns Fearchar an dannsa seo na òige.

Bonaidean Gorma, or as it was commonly known *Blue Bonnets*, is a dance set to the tune of *Scots Blue Bonnets*. This version presented here is as Farquar MacNeil performed the dance in his youth.

During the period when the dance was taught, a pair of slacks and a fisherman's jersey, complete with knitted Tam O' Shanter, would have been typical attire. Today the kilt may be worn if so desired.

Comharraichean — NOTES

An Ceòl / Music — The dance was and should be performed to the 6/8 time Jig *The Scots Blue Bonnets* (6 steps covering 96 bars). Not more than six steps is recommended for a demonstration.

Obair nan Làmh / Handwork — If danced in fisherman's attire, the arms are allowed to hang loosely at the sides (Hornpipe-type arm movements may be used, but must not be exaggerated). When danced by a girl, the skirt should be held lightly between thumb and forefinger of each hand throughout the dance.

Gluasadan sònraichte — SPECIAL MOVEMENTS

Ball of foot is used unless otherwise stated.

Skip-Change Step — As in Scottish Country Dancing, long and flowing but much higher on the feet and when changing direction (see 1st Step) a swivel action of balls of feet occur.

Shuffles — Single, Double or Treble Shuffles as to the dancers capability, but must be used consistently throughout the dance.

BREAKS

Leth-bhriseadh — HALF BREAK RF — (Danced on the Spot)
Bars
3   Extend RF to 4th Int. Aer. Pos. Low (and);
Spring on to RF, bringing LF to 3rd Rear Aer. Pos. Low off Right leg (not touching) (5);
Hop RF, extending LF to 4th Int. Aer. Pos. Low (and);
Hop RF, pointing LF in 5th Pos. (6);

4   Hop RF, extending LF to 4th Int. Aer. Pos. Low (and);
Spring LF, bringing RF to 3rd Rear Aer. Pos. Low off Left leg (not touching) (7);
Hop LF, extending RF to 4th Int. Aer. Pos. Low (and);
Hop LF, pointing RF in 5th Pos. (8).
Count: and 5 and 6, and 7 and 8

HALF BREAK LF
As for RF, but danced contra.

———o0o———

Briseadh — FULL BREAK RF
Bars
7   Spring on to balls of both feet in 1st Pos. (5);
Swivel on balls of both, twisting Heels outward (feet now in
an open inverted position) (and);
Twist Heels in-out (6);
Twist heels in-out (and);
Twist Heels in-out (a).
Count: 5 and 6 and a

8   Spring on to both feet, RF in 5th Pos. (7);
Execute a change, landing with LF in 5th Pos. (8).
Count: 7 8

FULL BREAK LF
As for RF, but danced contra.

———o0o———

Tòiseachadh — INTRODUCTION

Bars

1 - 4   Stand in Hebridean Starting Pos. (RF in front) with Arms at the sides.
Count: 1 2, 3 4, 5 6, 7 8.

5 - 6   Step to the right, close LF in front — Bow or Curtsey — Dèan modh — Count: 1 2, 3 4.

7 - 8   Step back to stand in Hebridean Starting Pos. (RF in front) — Count: 5 6, 7 8.

A' chiad cheum — FIRST STEP

Bars

1 - 2   With a disassemble on to LF dance one Skip-Change Step to RDF and then one Skip-Change;
Step on LF to LDF.
The diagonal is between 2nd Forward Pos. and 4th Int. Pos.
In this Step the Skip-Change Step is done thus:
Hop LF (and); Step RF diag. fwd (1); Close LF to 5th Rear Pos. (and);
Step RF slightly diag. fwd, swivel on R ball, sliding LF to 3rd Pos. (2);
then Hop-Step-Close-Step, Swivel to LD (and 3 and 4).
Count: and 1 and 2, and 3 and 4

3 - 4   HALF BREAK RF — Leth-bhriseadh.
Count: and 5 and 6, and 7 and 8

5 - 6   With a Hop LF to begin, repeat Bars 1 - 2.
Count: and 1 and 2, and 3 and 4

7 - 8   FULL BREAK RF — Briseadh.
Count: 5 and 6 and a, 7 8

9 -16   With a disassemble on to RF to begin, repeat Bars 1 - 8 contra.

53

An dara ceum — SECOND STEP

Bars

1   With a disassemble on to LF dance one Skip-Change Step to RDF (and 1 and 2).

2   Step LF (flat) diagonally backwards (3);
Step RF (flat) diagonally backwards (4) to regain starting position.
Count: and 1 and 2, 3 4

3 - 4   HALF BREAK LF — Leth-bhriseadh.
Count: and 5 and 6, and 7 and 8

5 - 6   With a Hop RF to begin, repeat Bars 1 - 2 contra.
Count: and 1 and 2, and 3 and 4

7 - 8   FULL BREAK RF — Briseadh.
Count: 5 and 6 and a, 7 8

9 -16   With a disassemble on to RF to begin, repeat Bars 1 - 8 contra.

An treas ceum — THIRD STEP

Bars

1   Spring on to both feet RF still in front (1);
Step on RF to 2nd Pos. (and);
Close LF to 5th Rear Pos. (2).

2   Hop LF, taking RF to 3rd Rear Aer. Pos. to begin, execute two Ceum cùl dùbailte with RF and LF (and 3 and 4).
    FIOS / NOTE: Try not to make the Ceum cùl dùbailte too bouncy!
    Count: 1 and 2, and 3 and 4

3 - 4   HALF BREAK RF — Leth-bhriseadh.
Count: and 5 and 6, and 7 and 8

5 - 6   Assemble LF in front to begin, repeat Bars 1 - 2 contra.
Count: 1 and 2, and 3 and 4

7 - 8   FULL BREAK LF — Briseadh.
         Count: 5 and 6 and a, 7 8

9 -16   Springing on to both feet LF still in front, repeat Bars 1 - 8
         contra.

An ceathramh ceum — FOURTH STEP

Bars

1 - 2   With a disassemble on to LF execute two Treble Shuffles
         springing LF then RF.
         Count: 1 and and a 2, 3 and and a 4
         FIOS / NOTE: These two Shuffles are at half normal speed,
         with an extension on counts 2 and 4.

3 - 4   HALF BREAK LF — Leth-bhriseadh.
         Count: and 5 and 6, and 7 and 8

5 - 6   With a Hop RF to begin, repeat Bars 1 - 2 contra.
         Count: 1 and and a 2, 3 and and a 4

7 - 8   FULL BREAK RF — Briseadh.
         Count: 5 and 6 and a, 7 8

9 -16   With an disassemble on to RF to begin, repeat Bars 1 - 8
         contra.

An còigeamh ceum — FIFTH STEP

Bars

1 - 2   Spring on to both feet RF still in 5th Pos. (1);
         Spread both feet to 2nd Pos. (and);
         Assemble LF in 5th Pos. (2);
         Change RF to 5th Pos. (3); Change LF to 5th Pos. (and);
         Change RF to 5th Pos. (4).
         Count: 1 and 2, 3 and 4

3 - 4   HALF BREAK RF — Leth-bhriseadh.
         Count: and 5 and 6, and 7 and 8

5 - 6   Repeat Bars 1 - 2.
          Count: 1 and 2, 3 and 4

7 - 8   FULL BREAK RF — Briseadh.
          Count: 5 and 6 and a, 7 8

9 -16   LF already in front, repeat Bars 1 - 8 contra.

An t-siathamh ceum — SIXTH STEP

Bars

1   Disassemble and then hop on LF, execute a Toe and Heel
          movement with RF in 5th Pos. (1 and);
          Assemble LF in 5th Pos. (2);

2   With a Hop RF to begin, repeat Bar 1 contra. (3 and 4).
          Count: 1 and 2, 3 and 4

3 - 4   HALF BREAK RF — Leth-bhriseadh.
          Count: and 5 and 6, and 7 and 8

5 - 6   Repeat Bars 1 - 2.
          Count: 1 and 2, 3 and 4

7 - 8   FULL BREAK RF — Briseadh.
          Count: 5 and 6 and a, 7 8

9 -16   With a disassemble on to RF, repeat Bars 1 - 8 contra.

Ceum air-leth — EXTRA STEP

Bars

1 - 2   Hopping on LF, execute a Shake-Shake-Down movement
          with RF (1 and 2);
          Shake-Shake-Down movement with LF (3 and 4).
          Count: 1 and 2, 3 and 4

3 - 4   HALF BREAK RF — Leth-bhriseadh.
          Count: and 5 and 6, and 7 and 8

56

| 5 - 6 | Repeat Bars 1 - 2. |
| | Count: 1 and 2, 3 and 4 |

| 7 - 8 | FULL BREAK RF — Briseadh. |
| | Count: 5 and 6 and a, 7 8 |

| 9 -16 | With a disassemble on to RF, repeat Bars 1 - 8 contra. |

A' Chrìoch — FINISH

Step to 2nd Pos. on RF, Close LF to RF in Hebridean Starting Pos. (flat) and Bow or Curtsey — Dèan modh.

Scotch Measure
(A Solo Hornpipe)

An Ceòl: The Hornpipe *Twa Bonnie Maidens.*
Tempo: 38 Bars per minute. Crotchet = 76 per minute.
Time: 2/4, 8-Bar Introduction. 16 Bars to each step.
Count: 2 Counts to each Bar.

Tomhas Beag

Seo fear dhe na dannsaichean as sinne, le gluasad sìmplidh agus beul-aithriseach. Tha an seòrsa briseadh àraid a th' ann ga chomharrachadh mar seo. Chan eil gluasad-làmhan idir ann. Tha e air a dhannsa leis a' phort *Two Bonnie Maidens.*

This version of *Scotch Measure* is as danced by Farquar MacNeil of Barra in his youth. The dance was never treated as anything special and the title merely suggests that it is a Scottish Dance — a 'Scotch Measure.' The dance is performed in a relaxed manner. Farquar always thought of the dance to be a 'girls' dance. The advanced variations of the steps are used if being performed by a man. There are no arm movements to this dance. Girls would hold their skirts, and the men have their arms hanging loose by the side or behind their backs.

Na Comharraichean — NOTES

An Ceòl / Music — The dance was performed to the Hornpipe *Twa Bonnie Maidens.* The Pipe Tune *Dornoch Links* is a good alternative tune.

Gluasadan sònraichte — SPECIAL MOVEMENTS

Briseadh — BREAK RF (also danced LF).
Bars

5 With feet parallel; Hop LF (land flat), and beat R ball (1); Still standing on LF flat, beat R ball again (and); Spring on to RF, repeat counts '1 and' with LF (ball) (2 and)

6 Repeat Bar 5, begin with springing on to LF and beating R ball. (3 and 4 and).

7	Jump both feet in place in 1st Pos. with only a slight raise of the heels from the ground. (5);
	Twist both heels out (and);
	Twist heels in-out (6); twist heels in-out (and); twist heels in-out (and).
	Slow, Slow, Quick, Quick, Quick
8	Assemble RF in 5th Pos. (7); execute a change and land with LF in 5th Pos. (8).
	Count: 1 and 2 and, 3 and 4 and, 5 and 6 and and, 7 8

Obair nan Làmh / Handwork: Arms hanging by the sides or hands clasped together behind body.

FIOS / NOTE: If executed by a girl **Bar 7** can be executed as follows:

Jump LF in 1st Pos. flat, placing RF in 4th Midway Pos. on ball (with Heel only slightly lifted off ground) (5);

Twist R heel out (and);

Twist R heel in-out (6); twist R heel in-out (and); twist R heel in-out (and).

Slow, Slow, Quick, Quick, Quick

The twisting actions can, as an alternative, be done the other way around, i.e.   Twist: out-in-out-in...
    5   and   6   and...

Briseadh — Break LF:
Same as above, but danced contra.

Foot Positions: Parallel when twisted out

The Break in this dance is in a peculiar pattern, characteristic only to this dance. It is done as follows:

1st	Step:	RF	—	LF
2nd	Step:	LF	—	RF
3rd	Step:	RF	—	LF
4th	Step:	LF	—	RF
5th	Step:	RF	—	LF
6th	Step:	RF	—	LF

Tòiseachadh — INTRODUCTION

Bars

1 - 4   Stand with Head, Arms and Feet in Hebridean Starting Pos.

5 - 8   Step to the Right, closing LF in front, Bow and Curtsey (dèan modh) slowly, step back to
original position (RF in front).

A' chiad cheum — FIRST STEP

Bars

1   With a slight Hop LF (and);
Step on to RF (flat) diagonally forward right (the diagonal is between 4th Int. and 2nd Forward Pos) (1);
Close LF (flat) in 3rd Rear Pos. (and);
Swivel on balls of both feet so LF lands in 3rd Pos. (2).

2   With a Hop RF to begin, repeat Bar 1 contra. (and 3 and 4).

3 - 4   Repeat Bars 1 - 2.
Count: and 1 and 2, and 3 and 4, and 5 and 6, and 7 and 8

5 - 8   BREAK RF — Briseadh.

9 - 12   Repeat Bars 1 - 4 contra.

13-16   BREAK LF — Briseadh.

An dara ceum — SECOND STEP

Bars

1 - 2   With a Hop LF, lift RF up to 3rd Aer. Pos. (1);
Hop LF, passing RF with a round-the-leg action to 3rd Rear Aer. Pos. (2);
Assemble RF in 5th Pos. (3);
Step RF towards 2nd Pos. on ball (and);
Close LF in to 5th Rear Pos. (4).

| 3 - 4 | With a Spring RF to begin, repeat Bars 1 - 2 contra. |
| | Count: 1 2, 3 and 4, 5 6, 7 and 8 |

| 5 - 8 | BREAK **LF** — Briseadh. |

| 9 -12 | Begin Hop RF, repeat Bars 1 - 4 contra. |

| 13-16 | BREAK **RF** — Briseadh. |

An dara ceum air-leth — SECOND STEP ADVANCED

Bars

1 - 2	With a Hop LF, lift RF up to 3rd Aer. Pos. (1);
	Hop LF, passing RF with a round-the-leg action to 3rd Rear Aer. Pos. (and);
	Hop LF, passing RF with a round-the-leg action to 3rd Aer. Pos. (2);
	Hop LF, passing RF with a round-the-leg action to 3rd Rear Aer. Pos. (and);
	Assemble RF in 5th Pos. (3);
	Step RF towards 2nd Pos. on ball (and);
	Close LF in to 5th Rear Pos. (4).

| 3 - 4 | With a Spring RF to begin, repeat Bars 1 - 2 contra. |
| | Count: 1 and 2 and, 3 and 4, 5 and 6 and, 7 and 8 |

| 5 - 8 | BREAK **LF** — Briseadh. |

| 9 -12 | Begin Hop RF, repeat Bars 1 - 4 contra. |

| 13-16 | BREAK **RF** — Briseadh. |

An treas ceum — THIRD STEP

Bars

1 - 2	Assemble with RF in 5th Pos. (1);
	Spread both feet towards 2nd Pos. on balls (and);
	Assemble LF in 5th Pos. (2);

Execute three changes in 5th Pos. RF, LF, RF in front respectively (3 and 4).

3 - 4 Change to LF in front to begin, repeat Bars 1 - 2 contra.
Count: 1 and 2, 3 and 4, 5 and 6, 7 and 8

5 - 8 BREAK RF — Briseadh.

9 -12 Repeat Bars 1 - 4 contra.

13-16 BREAK LF — Briseadh.

An treas ceum air-leth — THIRD STEP ADVANCED
Bars
1 - 2 Assemble with RF in 5th Pos. (1);
Spread both feet towards 2nd Pos. on balls (and);
Assemble LF in 5th Pos. (2);
Change RF to 5th Pos. (3);
Spread both feet towards 2nd Pos. on balls (and);
Assemble RF in 5th Pos. (4).

3 - 4 Change to LF in front, repeat Bars 1 - 2 contra.
Count: 1 and 2, 3 and 4, 5 and 6, 7 and 8

5 - 8 BREAK RF — Briseadh.

9 -12 Repeat Bars 1 - 4 contra.

13-16 BREAK LF — Briseadh.

An ceathramh ceum — FOURTH STEP
Bars
1 - 2 With a Spring on to LF, point RF in 2nd Pos (1);
Hop LF, take RF to 3rd Rear Aer. Pos. (and);
Spring RF, point LF in 2nd Pos. (2); Hop RF, take LF to 3rd
Aer. Pos. (and); Hop RF, point LF in 2nd Pos. (3);

Hop RF, take LF to 3rd Rear Aer. Pos. (and);
Spring LF, point RF in 2nd Pos. (4);
Hop LF, take RF to 3rd Aer. Pos. (and).

3   With a Spring RF, pointing LF in 3rd Rear Pos. to begin,
        execute 4 Rocks (5 and 6 and).

4   Step LF (flat) in place and execute a Shake action with RF
        towards 4th Midway Pos. going from normal to high level
        (7 and a);
        Step RF in 3rd Crossed Pos. execute a Pivot Turn to the left 8.
        Count: 1 and 2 and, 3 and 4 and, 5 and 6 and, 7 and a 8

5 - 8   BREAK **LF** — Briseadh.

9 - 12 Repeat Bars 1 - 4 contra.

13 - 16 BREAK **RF** — Briseadh.

An còigeamh ceum — FIFTH STEP

Bars

1 - 2   Assemble RF in 5th Pos. (1);
        Step RF towards 2nd Pos. (and);
        Close LF in to 5th Rear Pos. (2);
        Raise RF to a 3rd Aer. Pos. Low and springing RF,
        LF, RF execute three Backstep movements.
        (3 and 4).

   FIOS / NOTE: The round-the-leg movement is in a low aerial position.

3 - 4   Repeat Bars 1 - 2 contra.
        Count: 1 and 2, 3 and 4, 5 and 6, 7 and 8

5 - 8   BREAK RF — Briseadh.

9 -12   Repeat Bars 1 - 4 contra.

13-16   BREAK LF — Briseadh.

An t-siathamh ceum — SIXTH STEP

Bars

1 - 16   Same as in An còigeamh ceum / Fifth Step but during the
Backsteps a complete turn on the spot is made. When travelling
to the right the turn is made clockwise and when travelling to the
left the turn is anti-clockwise.

A' Chrìoch — FINISH

Step to 2nd Pos. on RF, Close LF to RF in Hebridean Starting Pos. (flat)
and Bow or Curtsey — Dèan modh.

Till a-rithist
Aberdonian Lassie
(A Solo Dance)

An Ceòl: *The Quakers' March.*
Tempo: 50 Bars per minute. Crotchet = 100 per minute.
Time: 6/8, 8-Bar Introduction. 16 Bars to each step.
Count: 2 Counts to each Bar.

A rèir rannsachadh le Ceit Anna NicFhionghuin rinn Eoghan MacLachlainn suas an dannsa seo do bhan-sgoilear a bha teagasg ann an Uibhist a Deas. Bha ia' fàgail Uibhist 's a' tilleadh dhachaigh a dh'Obar-Dheathain.

Chithear le ainm an dannsa, gu robhar ro-mheasail oirre san Eilean agus gu robh dòchas ann gun tilleadh i a-rithist. Tha e air a dhannsa le na puirt *The Quaker* agus *The Quaker's Wife.*

Aberdonian Lassie is an interesting dance in that, it has the character of a 'Fling' arrangement and consists of six set steps, but also includes certain movements closely related to step dancing. Our knowledge of this dance stems from Farquar MacNeil. The dance seems only to have been known on the Isle of Barra. The dance is known under its alternative Gaelic name today on Barra and South Uist — *Till a-rithist* (Come Back Again).

The tunes running with this dance are the 6/8 Marches *The Quake* andthe very similar tune the *The Quaker's Wife*. Either fits the dance to perfection.

According to the research of Katie Ann Mackinnon, there is a story saying that Ewen MacLachlan devised this dance in honour of a woman, a teacher from Aberdeen, who had been living and teaching in Bornish on South Uist for a very long time. She was apparently very well liked, and upon her departure for home, this dance was devised in the hope that she would return — Come back again. It has also been suggested that the wish for somebody to return relates to the Jacobite Clansmens' wish for Bonnie Prince Charlie to come back.

Comharraichean — NOTES
An Ceòl / Music — The dance is performed to the March *The Quakers' March*. As an alternative tune the slightly different tune *The Quaker's Wife* may be used.

Gluasadan sònraichte — SPECIAL MOVEMENTS

Ball of foot is used unless otherwise stated.

Ceum cùl dùbailte — Hop-backsteps or retirés.

Heel - Toe - Beat — With RF: Beat R Heel in 2nd Pos. (1); Beat RF on ball in 2nd Pos. (and); Beat LF on ball in place (a). If a sideways movement occurs (2nd Step), the supporting foot (LF above) moves into 3rd Rear Pos. on the beat (a). Count '1 and a'. Repeat as required. The beats with heel and ball should be strongly accented.

Highland Fling Turn

Shakes — The shakes should, when reaching their highest point, be slightly lower than a High Aerial Position.The shakes are strongly accented in this dance without being stiff in movement.

TURN R.

Bars

7   With a Hop RF, point LF in 2nd Pos. (5);
           Making a Half Turn to the right, Hop RF, taking LF to
           3rd Rear Aer. Pos. (6).

8   With a Hop RF, point LF in 2nd Pos. (7);
           Hop RF, bringing LF to 3rd Aer. Pos. (8).
           The whole movement is: Side, Behind (1/2 turn),
           Side, In front.
           Count: 5 6, 7 8
     Obair nan Làmh / Handwork — 1st Pos. on Bar 72nd Pos. R on
           Bar 8. (Opposite arm to working foot.)

Turn L

Bars

15 - 16   Same as above, but danced contra.

This dance is performed facing the front during Bars 1 - 6. Making a half turn on Bars 7 - 8. Facing the back on Bars 9 - 14. Making a half turn on Bars 15 - 16. The idea is to travel forwards and backwards whenever possible or whenever stated.

The dance is ideal to perform in a room or hall with the audience sitting right round the dancer.

Tòiseachadh — INTRODUCTION

Bars

1 - 4   Stand in Hebridean Starting Pos. (RF in front) with Arms at
the sides.
Count: 1 2, 3 4, 5 6, 7 8.

5 - 6   Step to the right, closing LF in front — Bow or Curtsey —
Dèan modh — Count: 1 2, 3 4.

7 - 8   Step back to stand in Hebridean Starting Pos. (RF in front) —
Count: 5 6, 7 8.

A' chiad cheum — FIRST STEP
'Side. behind, Toe and Heel'

Bars

Travelling straight forward on Bars 1 - 6 and back to place
during Bars 9 - 14:

1 - 2   With a Hop LF, Point RF in 2nd Pos. (1);
Hop LF, taking RF to 3rd Rear Aer. Pos. (2);
Spring RF, Point LF in 2nd Pos. (3);
Hop RF, taking LF to 3rd Rear Aer. Pos. (4).
Count: 1 2, 3 4

Obair nan Làmh / Handwork — 2nd Pos. in opposition, changing
between counts '2' and '3'.

3 - 4   Hop RF twice, making a Toe and Heel Movement in 5th Pos.
with LF (5 6); Spring then Hop LF making a Toe and Heel
Movement in 5th Pos. with RF. (7 8).
Count: 5 6, 7 8

Obair nan Làmh / Handwork — 1st Pos.

5 - 6   With a Spring RF, Repeat Bars 1 - 2 contra.
Count: 1 2, 3 4

Obair nan Làmh / Handwork — 2nd Pos. in opposition changing
between counts '2' and '3'.

| 7 - 8 | TURN R. |
| | Count: 5 6, 7 8 |

9 - 14   With a Hop RF to begin, repeat Bars 1 - 6 contra.

15-16   TURN L.

An dara ceum — SECOND STEP
'Heel, Toe, Beat'

Bars

1 - 2   With a Hop LF, point RF in 2nd Pos. (Hold Pos. as long as possible!) (1);
'Quickly' Hop LF, bringing RF to 3rd Rear Aer. Pos. (and);
Make an Heel-Toe-Beat Movement with RF moving towards 2nd Pos. (2 and a);
Heel-Toe-Beat Movement RF again moving towards 2nd Pos. (3 and a);
Beat R Heel in 2nd Pos. (4);
Beat RF on Toe in 2nd Pos. (and). (Very slight pause).
Count: 1 and, 2 and a, 3 and a, 4 and

Obair nan Làmh / Handwork — 2nd Pos. in opposition.

3 - 4   With a Spring RF, repeat Bars 1 - 2 with contra.
Count: 5 and, 6 and a, 7 and a, 8 and

5 - 6   With a Spring LF, repeat Bars 1 - 2.

7 - 8   TURN R.

9 -16   With a Hop RF to begin. Repeat Bars 1 - 8 contra.

FIOS / NOTE: In this step it is essential that the dancer listens to the music and dances with it. The music tells you when to do slight pauses and drag the movements out.

An treas ceum — THIRD STEP
'Shake and Travel'

Bars

1 - 2   With a Hop LF, point RF in 2nd Pos (1);
Hop LF, taking RF to 3rd Rear Aer. Pos. (2);
Hop LF, making a round-the-leg movement with RF to 3rd
Aer. Pos. (3);
Hop LF, executing a Shake action with RF to a (almost high)
4th Int. Aer. Pos. (and 4).
Count: 1 2, 3 and 4

Obair nan Làmh / Handwork — 2nd Pos. L .

3 - 4   Spring RF, point LF in 5th Pos. (5); Hop RF, execute a Shake
Action with LF to a (almost high)
4th Int. Aer. Pos. (and 6); Assemble LF in 3rd Rear Pos. (bent
knees) (7);

glide RF towards 2nd Pos. (and); Slide LF to assemble in 5th Pos. (bent knees) (8).

FIOS / NOTE: The travel towards 2nd Pos. should be a sliding movement, high upon toes, with feet in contact with the floor all the time. No extensions prior to assemble.

Count: 5 and 6, 7 and 8

Obair nan Làmh / Handwork — Man: 3rd Pos. Woman: 5th Pos. on counts '5 and 6'. Bring outside of hands towards each other in 5th Pos; Raise arms upwards and out through 4th and 3rd positions and down to 5th again in a Seann Triubhas-like circling movement during counts'7 and 8'.

5 - 6   With a Spring LF, repeat Bars 3 - 4 contra.

7 - 8   TURN R.
            Count: 1 and 2, 3 and 4, 5 6, 7 8

9 -16   With a Hop RF to begin. Repeat Bars 1 - 8 contra.

An ceathramh ceum — FOURTH STEP
'Ceum cùl dùbailte (and Heel, Toe, Beat)'

Bars

1 - 2   With a Hop LF, point RF in 2nd Pos. (1);
            Hop LF, bringing RF to 3rd Rear Aer. Pos. (2);
            Hop LF to begin, keeping RF in 3rd Rear Aer. Pos.,
            Dance 2 Ceum cùl dùbailte RF and LF (and 3 and 4).
            Finish with LF in 3rd Rear Pos.
            Count: 1 2, and 3 and 4

Obair nan Làmh / Handwork — 2nd Pos. L on Bar 1.
3rd Pos. on Bar 2.

3 - 4   Spring RF, execute Heel-Toe-Beat-Heel-Toe Movement in Open 3rd Pos. with LF (5 and a 6 and a).
            Spring LF, execute Heel-Toe-Beat-Heel-Toe Movement in Open 3rd Pos. with RF(7 and a 8 and a).
            There is **no** travel in the Heel-Toe-Beat... Movement.
            Count: 5 and a 6 and a, 7 and a 8 and a

Obair nan Làmh / Handwork — 2nd Pos. in opposition.

5 - 6   With a Spring RF, repeat Bars 1 - 2 contra.

7 - 8   TURN R.
             Count: 1 2, 3 and 4 and, 5 6, 7 8

9 -16   With a Hop RF to begin, repeat Bars 1 - 8 contra.

                   An còigeamh ceum — FIFTH STEP
              'Assemble, Travel Backwards and Ceum cùl dùbailte'
Bars
1 - 2   With a Hop LF, point RF in 2nd Pos (1);
             Hop LF, taking RF to 3rd Rear Aer. Pos. (2);
             Hop LF, making a round-the-leg movement with RF to 3rd
             Aer. Pos. (3);
             Hop LF, executing a Shake action with RF to a (almost high)
             4th Int. Aer. Pos. (and 4).
             Count: 1 2, 3 and 4
             Obair nan Làmh / Handwork — 2nd Pos. L .

3 - 4   Assemble RF in 5th Pos. (bent knees) (5);
             Step RF to 4th Rear Pos. (straight backwards) (and);
             Step LF in 5th Pos. ('Assemble', bent knees) (6);
             Keep weight on LF to finish.
             Hop LF to begin, lift RF to 3rd Rear Aer. Pos., Dance 2 Ceum
             cùl dùbailte RF and LF (and 7 and 8).
             Finish with LF in 3rd Rear Pos.
             Count: 5 and 6, and 7 and 8
             Obair nan Làmh / Handwork — 3rd Pos.

5 - 6   Assemble LF in 5th Pos. (bent knees) (5);
             Step LF to 4th Rear Pos. (straight backwards) (and);
             Step RF in 5th Pos. ('Assemble', bent knees) (2);
             Keep weight on RF to finish.
             Hop RF to begin, lift LF to 3rd Rear Aer. Pos., Dance 2 Ceum
             cùl dùbailte LF and RF
             (and 3 and 4).
             Finish with RF in 3rd Rear Pos.
             Count: 1 and 2, and 3 and 4
             Obair nan Làmh / Handwork — 3rd Pos.

                                                              71

7 - 8   TURN R.
         Count: 5 6, 7 8

9 - 16   With a Hop RF to begin. Repeat Bars 1 - 8 contra.
         FIOS / NOTE: The step taken backwards involved in Bars 3 and 5 should
         be fairly short — about the length of a foot.

An siathamh ceum — SIXTH STEP
'Point, Turn and Rock'

Bars

1 - 2   With a Hop LF, Point RF in 2nd Pos. (1);
         Hop LF, bring RF to 3rd Rear Aer. Pos. (2);
         Spring RF, Point LF in 2nd Pos. (3);
         Hop RF, bring LF to 3rd Rear Aer. Pos. (4).
         Count: 1 2, 3 4
Obair nan Làmh / Handwork — 2nd Pos. in opposition.

3 - 4   Spring LF, pointing RF in 2nd Pos. to begin, execute a
         Highland Fling Turn to the Left on the spot.
         Finish with RF in 3rd Rear Aer. Pos.
         Count: 5 6, 7 8
Obair nan Làmh / Handwork — 1st Pos.

5 - 6   With a Hop LF, bring RF on the point to 5th Rear Pos. (1);
         Execute 3 Rocks, springing RF, LF, RF.
         Count: 1 2, 3 4
Obair nan Làmh / Handwork: 3rd Pos.

7 - 8   TURN R.
         Count: 5 6, 7 8
9 -16   With a Hop RF to begin. Repeat Bars 1 - 8 contra.

A' Chrìoch — FINISH
Step to 2nd Pos. on RF, Close LF to RF in Hebridean Starting Pos. (flat)
and Bow or Curtsey — Dèan modh.

Lusan Dhùn Eideann
The Flowers of Edinburgh
(A Solo Step Dance)

An Ceòl: *The Flowers of Edinburgh.*
Tempo: 54 Bars per minute.
Time: 2/4, 8-Bar Introduction. 16 Bars to each step.
Count: 2 Counts to each Bar.

'S e dannsa aon-neach tha seo le sia ceuman. Tha e air a dhannsa leis a' phort *Lusan Dhùn Eideann.* Tha comharradh sònraichte anns an dannsa seo agus 's e sin gu bheil thu a' gluasad le crathadh nan cas, agus a' dèanamh a' bhriseadh le cuartag air an spot.

This is a dance with a rather confusing background. Actually we have two separate types of dance bearing the same title, one hard shoe step- or tap-dance, and the other a soft shoe step-dance, with the character of a *Highland Laddie* type of dance. The soft shoe version is probably just a selection of movements fitted to the tune *Flowers of Edinburgh.* Its characteristics are the flowing nature of the steps and the 'Shake and Pivot' at the end of each eight-bar phrase. Of great interest to us is to Note that this dance is found under the name of *Highland Laddie*, and also performed to the tune of the same name in the book **Some Traditional Scottish Dances** by G. Douglas Taylor, which was published in 1929. This strongly suggests that this is another *Highland Laddie* but set to the tune *Flowers of Edinburgh.* This is the surviving style in the Hebrides today, and the Sgoil Dhannsa nan Eileanach call their version *Lusan Dhùn Eideann* in Gaelic.

Na Comharraichean — NOTES

Obair nan Làmh / Handwork — The man would raise opposite arm to working foot; 3rd Pos. is used when travelling sideways and when executing Back Steps and High Cuts. When danced by a girl, the skirt should be held lightly between thumb and forefinger of each hand throughout the dance.

Gluasadan sònraichte — SPECIAL MOVEMENTS

Ball of foot is used unless otherwise stated.

Shake-Shake-Down — With RF — Hop on LF, extending RF with a Shake action to 4th Int. Aer. Pos. (1); Hop LF, bringing RF in then re-extending it with a Shake action to 2nd Aer. Pos. (and); Spring both feet together with RF in 5th Rear Pos. (2).

Also with LF, but danced contra.

Pivot L
Bars
7 - 8   Spring (or Step) LF in place extending RF to 4th Int. Aer. Pos. (5);
Execute a Shake action with RF to 4th Int. Aer. Pos. (and 6);
Bringing RF to 3rd Crossed Pos., Pivot to Left on balls of both feet, finishing with LF in 5th Pos. (7 8).
Count: 5 and 6, 7 8

Pivot R
As Pivot L, but danced contra.

Tòiseachadh — INTRODUCTION

Bars
1 - 4   Stand in Hebridean Starting Pos. (RF in front) with Arms in 1st Pos. — Count: 1 2, 3 4, 5 6, 7 8.

5 - 6   Step to the right, closing LF in front — Bow or Curtsey — Dèan modh — Count: 1 2, 3 4.

7 - 8   Step back to stand in Hebridean Starting Pos. (RF in front) — Count: 5 6, 7 8.

74

A' chiad cheum — FIRST STEP

Bars

1 - 2   Disassemble on to LF, pointing RF in 5th Pos. and
immediately extending it to 4th Int. Aer. Pos. (1 and);
Hop LF, execute a Shake Action with the RF. (a 2);
Spring RF, repeat Counts 1and a 2 with LF
(3 and a 4).
Count: 1 and a 2, 3 and a 4

3 - 4   Dance a Shake, Shake, Down Movement with LF (5 and 6);
Dance a Shake, Shake, Down Movement with RF (7 and 8).
Count: 5 and 6, 7 and 8

5 - 6   Repeat Bars 1 - 2
Count: 1 and a 2, 3 and a 4

7 - 8   Pivot L
Count: 5 and 6, 7 8

9 - 16   With a disassemble on to RF, repeat Bars 1 - 8 contra.
Obair nan Làmh / Handwork — Opposite 2nd Pos. to working
foot.

An dara ceum — SECOND STEP

Bars

1 - 2   Raise RF to 3rd Aer. Pos., dance 3 Backsteps, springing on to
RF to begin. (1 2, 3);
Step LF to Forward 2nd Pos. and close RF to 5th Rear Pos.
(and 4).
Count : 1 2, 3 and 4

3 - 4   Repeat Bars 1-2 contra.
(Count: 5 6, 7 and 8)

5 - 6   Repeat Bars 1-2.
(Count: 1 2, 3 and 4)

7 - 8   Pivot L .
             Count: 5 and 6, 7 8
9 - 16   Repeat Bars 1 - 8 contra.
    Obair nan Làmh / Handwork — 3rd Position for Backsteps
             (Counts '1 2, 3');
             2nd Position in opposition (Counts 'and 4').
    FIOS / NOTE — The Backsteps and the sideways travel must be smooth
             and flowing. Knees must be relaxed.

                    An treas ceum — THIRD STEP
Bars
1 - 2   With a Spring on to LF to begin, dance a 'Fling' turn to the
             Left.
             Count: 1 2, 3 4

3 - 4   Hop LF, bringing RF with a round-the-leg movement to 3rd
             Aer. Pos.,
             Step RF to Forward 2nd Pos.,
              Close LF to 5th Rear Pos. (5 and 6); Spring on to RF,
             bringing LF to 3rd Aer. Pos.,
             Step LF to Forward 2nd Pos.,
             Close RF in 5th Rear Pos. (7 and 8).
             Count: 5 and 6, 7 and 8

5 - 6   With a disassemble on to LF, execute a Point-Close-Beat
             movement with RF (1 and 2);
             Spring RF, Point-Close-Beat with LF (3 and4).
             Count: 1 and 2, 3 and 4

7 - 8   Pivot L .
             Count: 5 and 6, 7 8

9-16   Repeat Bars 1 - 8 contra.
    Obair nan Làmh / Handwork — 2nd Position in opposition.

76

An ceathramh ceum — FOURTH STEP

Bars

1-2   Moving to the right. Hop on LF, Place RF on toe sideways in 2nd Inverted Pos. (R knee turned in and touching L knee), Hop on LF, place RF on heel in 2nd Pos. (1 2); Repeat once more (3 4).
Count: 1 2, 3 4

3 - 4   Spring on to RF, taking LF to 3rd Aer. Pos. (5);
Step LF on heel towards 4th Int. Pos. (and);
Close RF in 3rd Rear Pos. (6);
Spring on to LF, taking RF to 3rd Aer. Pos. (7);
Step RF on heel towards 4th Int. Pos. (and);
Close LF in 3rd Rear Pos.(8).
Count: 5 and 6, 7 and 8

5 - 6   With a Spring RF to begin, repeat Bars 1 - 2 contra, moving to the left.
Count: 1 2, 3 4

7 - 8   Pivot L .
Count: 5 and 6, 7 8

9-16   With a disassemble on to RF to begin, repeat Bars 1 - 8 contra.

Obair nan Làmh / Handwork — 2nd Position in opposition.

An còigeamh ceum — FIFTH STEP

Bars

1 - 2   With a disassemble on to LF, point RF in 5th Pos, and immediately extending it to 4th Int. Aer.Pos. (1);
Hop LF, shake RF (and 2).
Spring RF and repeat counts '1 and 2' contra (3 and 4).
Count: 1 and 2, 3 and 4

3 - 4   Moving sideways to the left, step LF towards 2nd Pos. on ball and close RF in 5th Rear Pos. (and 1);
Step LF towards 2nd Pos. and close RF in 5th Pos. (and 2);
Step LF towards 2nd Pos. on ball and close RF in 5th Rear Pos. (and 3);
Step LF towards 2nd Pos. and close RF in 5th Pos. (and 4).
Count: and 1 and 2, and 3 and 4

5 - 6   With a disassemble on to LF, repeat Bars 1 - 2.
Count: 1 and 2, 3 and 4

7 - 8	Pivot L . Count: 5 and 6, 7 8

9-16   With a disassemble on to RF to begin, repeat Bars 1-8 contra.
   Obair nan Làmh / Handwork: 2nd Position in opposition on
   Bars 1 - 2 and 5 - 6. 3rd Position on Bars 3 - 4.

An t-siathamh ceum — SIXTH STEP

Bars

1 - 2   With a disassemble on to RF, then springing LF, RF, LF,
   execute 4 High Cuts.
   Count: 1 2, 3 4

3 - 4   With a Spring RF, point LF to 2nd Pos. (5);
   Hop RF, bringing LF to 3rd Rear Aer. Pos. (6);
   Hop RF, execute a round-the-leg movement with LF to 3rd
   Aer. Pos. (7);
   Spring LF, simultaneously extending RF to 4th
   Int. Aer. Pos. (8).
   Count: 5 6, 7 8

5 - 6   With a Spring RF, pointing LF to 2nd Pos., execute a 'Fling'
   turn to the Right.
   Count: 1 2, 3 4

7 - 8   Pivot L .
   Count: 5 and 6, 7 8

9-16   With a disassemble on to LF to begin, repeat Bars 1-8 contra.
   Obair nan Làmh / Handwork — 3rd Position on Bars 1 - 2.
      2nd Position in opposition on Bars 3 - 6. On count '8' in
      Bar 4 L arm is in 2nd Pos.

A' Chrìoch — FINISH

Step to 2nd Pos. on RF, Close LF to RF in Hebridean Starting Pos.
(flat) and Bow or Curtsey — Dèan modh.

Miss Forbes
(A Ladies Solo Dance)

An Ceòl: *Wee Man at the Loom.*
Tempo: 48 - 50 Bars per minute.
Time: 2/4, 8-Bar Introduction.   16 Bars to each step.
Count: 2 Counts to each Bar.

'S e dannsa aon-neach boireannaich tha seo, le seachd ceumannan. Tha e air fear dhen fheadhainn mu dheireadh a chaidh a ghabhail a-staigh sa cho-chruinneachadh aig Dannsa nan Eileanach.

Miss Forbes is known in several versions, and these hail either from the Hebrides or from the North East. The version of the dance we have from Katie Ann Mackinnon has seven steps of which some are quite different in style from the mainland dance. The mainland versions all have five steps to them. Mrs Mackinnon claims that her version is not a dance taught by Ewen, but has come to the Islands at a later stage; she does not know, however, from where. It is not known to us who this Miss Forbes was. Quite likely she was a successful student of an Aberdeen-shire dancing-master who made a selection of steps for her.

Na Comharraichean — NOTES
An Ceòl / Music — The dance is best performed to the tune *Wee Man at the Loom.*

Obair nan Làmh / Handwork — Girls hold dress between the thumb and forefinger of each hand throughout the dance, if not otherwise stated.

Gluasadan sònraichte — SPECIAL MOVEMENTS

Ball of foot is used unless otherwise stated.
Ceum cùl dùbailte
Skip Change of Step — Hop on LF, extending RF to 4th Aer Pos. (and); Step RF in 4th Pos (1); Close LF to 5th Rear Pos (and); Step RF in 4th Pos. (2). Repeat with LF and as desired.

Syncopted Hops — With RF — Hop on LF, lifting R leg towards 4th Int. Aer. Pos. with bent knee and shin and foot hanging vertical and pointed (1); Place RF on half point in Open 5th Pos. (and); Beat LF in place (2). With LF — As for RF, but contra.

An Tòiseachadh — INTRODUCTION

Bars

1 - 4   Stand with Head, Arms and Feet in Hebridean Starting Pos.
         Count: 1 2, 3 4, 5 6, 7 8.

5 - 7   Step to the side on RF — Curtsey — Step back (RF in front)
         Count: 1 2, 3 4, 5 6

8   Make 1/8 turn Right.
         Count: 7 8.

A' chiad cheum — FIRST STEP

Bars

1 - 2   Making a 1/2 Circle by forward-right (anti-clockwise) dance
         two Skip Change Step Movements RF and LF.
         Count: and 1 and 2, and 3 and 4

3 - 4   At top, having R shoulder towards the front, Hop LF, then
         springing RF, LF, RF, execute 4 Shuffles.
         Count: 5 and 6 and, 7 and 8 and

5 - 6   With a Hop RF, repeat bars 1 - 2 contra, continuing the circle
         back to place.
         Finish facing the front.
         Count: and 1 and 2, and 3 and 4

7 - 8   Hop RF, then springing LF, RF, LF, execute 4 Shuffles.
         Count: 5 and 6 and, 7 and 8 and

9 - 16   Repeat Bars 1 - 8 contra, making a circle clockwise, starting forward-left.
Obair nan Làmh / Handwork — Hold skirt throughout the step.

An dara ceum — SECOND STEP

Bars

1 - 2   Dance two Syncopated Hops with RF.
Count: 1 and 2, 3 and 4

3 - 4   Step RF in 5th Pos. (5);
Step LF towards 4th Int. Rear Pos. (and);
Close RF to 5th Pos. (6);
Point LF to 4th Int. Rear Aer. **Low** Pos. (and);
Close LF in 5th Rear Pos. (7);
Step RF towards 4th Int. Pos. (and);
Close LF to 5th Rear Pos. (8).
Count: 5 and 6 and, 7 and 8

5 - 8   With a disassemble on to RF to begin, repeat Bars 1 - 4 contra.
Count: and 1 and 2, and 3 and 4, 5 and 6 and, 7 and 8

9 - 16   With a disassemble on to LF to begin, repeat Bars 1 - 8 contra.
Obair nan Làmh / Handwork — Hold skirt throughout the step.

An treas ceum — THIRD STEP

Bars

1 - 2   Place RF on Toe in Inverted 2nd Pos. (heel turned outwards and upwards with knee turned inwards), beat LF in place (and 1);
Turning Right knee outwards, place Heel of RF in 2nd Pos. and close LF to 3rd Rear Pos.(and 2);
Place RF on half-point in 2nd Pos and close LF to 5th Rear Pos. (and 3);
Step RF on Heel in 2nd Pos. and close LF in 3rd Rear Pos. (and 4).
Count: and 1 and 2, and 3 and 4

3 - 4   Hop LF to begin, dance three Ceum cùl dùbailte, stepping on to RF, LF and RF (and 5 and 6 and 7);
Step LF to 2nd Pos. and close RF to 5th Rear Pos. (and 8).
FIOS / NOTE: During the Ceum cùl dùbailte movements, right shoulder must be pulled back slightly, so that the backward movement involved will be towards the starting point.
Dancer faces front during the step-close on counts 'and 8.'
Count: and 5 and 6, and 7 and 8

5 - 8   Repeat Bars 1 - 4 contra.
Count: and 1 and 2, and 3 and 4, and 5 and 6, and 7 and 8

9 - 16   Repeat Bars 1 - 8.
Obair nan Làmh / Handwork — 2nd Pos. in opposition on Bars 1-2.
3rd Pos. for Ceum cùl dùbailte movements.
5th Pos. for Step, Close.

An ceathramh ceum — FOURTH STEP

Bars

1 - 2   Disassemble on to LF, placing RF in 3rd Aer. Pos. (1);
Hop LF, bringing RF with a round-the-leg action to 3rd Rear Aer. Pos. (2);
Hop LF, bringing RF with a round-the-leg action to 3rd Aer. Pos. (3);
Quick Hop LF, extending RF to 4th Int. Aer. Pos. (and);
Hop LF, placing RF in 3rd Aer. Pos. (4).
Count: 1 2, 3 and 4

3 - 4   With a Hop LF to begin, execute two Ceum cùl dùbailte stepping on to RF and LF (and 5 and 6);
With LF behind, execute a change landing with LF in 5th Pos.(7);
Execute two changes RF and LF in front respectively (and 8).
Count: and 5 and 6, 7 and 8

5 - 8   With a disassemble on to RF to begin, repeat Bars 1 - 4 contra.
Count: 1 2, 3 and 4, and 5 and 6, 7 and 8

9 - 16   Repeat Bars 1 - 8.
Obair nan Làmh / Handwork — Hold skirt throughout the step.

An còigeamh ceum — FIFTH STEP

Bars

1 - 2   Dance two Syncopated Hops with RF facing the front
(1 and 2, 3 and 4).

3 - 4   Making a halfway anti-clockwise turn on the spot, to finish
facing the rear.
Hop LF, lifting RF up behind and off L leg. (5);
Treble RF out-in, in 4th Int. Pos.;
Step RF in 3rd Pos. then beat LF in 3rd Rear Pos.
(and and a 6);
Treble RF out-in, in 4th Int. Pos.;
Step RF in 3rd Rear Pos. then beat LF in 3rd Pos.
(and and a 7);
Treble RF out-in, in 4th Int. Pos.;
Beat RF in 3rd Pos. then beat LF in 3rd Rear Pos.
(and and a 8).
Count: 1 and 2, 3 and 4, 5 and and a 6 and and, a 7
and and a 8

5 - 8   Repeat Bars 1 - 4, completing the turn to face the front.
Count: 1 and 2, 3 and 4, 5 and and a 6 and and, a 7
and and a 8

9 -16   With a Spring RF to begin, repeat Bars 1 - 8 making a
complete clockwise turn.
Obair nan Làmh / Handwork — Opposite arm to working foot
raised in 2nd Pos., the other holding skirt.

An t-siathamh ceum — SIXTH STEP

Bars

1 - 2   Making 1/8 turn to the Right, Pas de Basque RF (1 and 2);
Hop RF bringing LF to 3rd Aer. Pos. Low, Step LF, bringing

RF to 3rd Rear Aer. Pos. Low (and 3);
Hop LF and bring RF down to 5th Rear Pos. (and 4).
Count: 1 and 2, and 3 and 4

3 - 4   Making 1/8 turn to the Left, repeat Bars 1 - 2 contra.
Count: 5 and 6, and 7 and 8

5 - 6   Repeat Bars 1 - 2, making a complete turn to the right
on the spot.
Count: 1 and 2, and 3 and 4

5 - 8   Facing front, execute four Shuflles springing LF, RF, LF, RF.
Count: 5 and 6 and, 7 and 8 and

9 - 16   Making 1/8 turn to the Left, repeat Bars 1 - 8 contra
Obair nan Làmh / Handwork — Hold skirt throughout the step.

An t-seachdamh ceum — SEVENTH STEP

Bars

1 - 2   Hop LF, pointing RF in 5th Pos. (1);
Hop LF, execute a Shake movement with RF to 4th Int. Aer.
Pos. (and 2);
Step RF in 3rd Rear Pos. on ball (3);
Step LF in 3rd Rear Pos. on ball (and);
Step (beat) RF in 3rd Pos. on ball (4) (Step-Step-Step, no
hops or springs!).
Count: 1 and 2, 3 and 4

3 - 4   Step LF on ball to 4th Int. Pos. (and);
Close RF to 5th Rear Pos. (5);
Step LF on ball to 4th Int. Pos. (and);
Close RF to 5th Rear Pos. (6);
Point LF in 4th Int. Pos. (and);
Hop RF to begin, execute two Ceum cùl dùbailte stepping on
to LF and RF, moving RDB to starting position (a 7 and 8).
Count: and 5 and 6 and, a 7 and 8

5 - 8   With a Hop RF to begin, repeat Bars 1 - 4 contra.
          Count: 1 and 2, 3 and 4, and 5 and 6 and, a 7 and 8

9 - 16   Repeat Bars 1 - 8.

A' Chrìoch — FINISH

Step to 2nd Pos. on RF, Close LF to RF in Hebridean Starting Pos. and
Curtsey — Dèan modh.

Caisteal Chiosamul
(Kismul Castle)

Chaidh *Caisteal Chiosamul* a chur ri chèile le Fearchar MacNèill, mar chuimhneachan air Maighstir Iain Mac a' Mhaolain à Barraigh. Bha Maighstir Iain ro-dhèidheil air Dannsa Nan Eileanach, agus bha deòin-bhàidh dhùrachdach aige gum biodh iad air an cumail beò, agus air an dannsa gun atharrachadh ach mar a bha iad bho thùs.

Thug Fearchar bliadhnaichean a' suidheachadh ceumannan an dannsa seo, mun deach a dhannsa airson a' chiad uair aig Fèis Bharraigh anns a' bhliadhna naoi ceud deug ceithir fichead 's a seachd (1987). Thug e cuideachd stiùireadh bho iomadach freumh mun do chuir e ri chèile. Chan e dannsa co-fharpais tha seo idir. 'S ann a-mhàin airson sealladh agus toil-inntinn a tha e ri bhith air a dhannsa.

Tha an dannsa air leth annasach a chionn 's gu bheil an làmh 's a' chas air an aon taobh ag obair còmhla. Tha e cuideachd cho innleachdach air a chur air dòigh 's gu faod aon duine, no dithis, no triùir, no barrachd a dhannsa. An seo, thathar ga shealltainn airson dithis — ach — ma bhios aon duine no triùir ga dhannsa, nì an neach a tha na aonar ceuman a''pholka' leis fhèin.

Sgeulachd An Dannsa

Tha thu dol gu 'Cuirm' dhan Chaisteal sa bhàgh. Tha thu ag iomradh tarsainn an uisge. Tha thu gnogadh aig doras a' Chaisteil. Tha an doras ga fhosgladh. Tha thu air d' fhàilteachadh a-steach. Caithidh tu an oidhche gu h-aighearach, le biadh is deoch, cèol is dannsa.

Mar bu dual nuair a bhiodh a' 'Chuirm' seachad rachadh an trumpaidear suas gu balla-dìonaidh a' chaisteil agus dh'èigheadh e:- "Tha MacNèill deiseil dhe bhiadh, faodaidh Prionnsaichean an t-saoghail a-nis suidhe sìos a dh'ithe."

Tha thu an sin a' fàgail a' chaisteil, a' togail do làimh san dealachadh, agus ag iomradh air ais gu tìr.

Caisteal Chiosamul
(Kismul Castle)

The Dance was made by Farquar MacNeil of Barra as a tribute to the memory of Father John MacMillan of Barra. Father MacMillan was a purist in everything concerning the Gaelic traditions of the islands; its music, dance and language.

Farquar MacNeil started devising this dance many years ago when still living in Ayr on the mainland. As time passed he added more and more to it, until it developed to its present form. Moving back to Barra some years ago, he decided to have it performed at Fèis Bharraigh in 1987.

The story of the dance
The dance tells a story of a couple rowing out to the castle in the bay to attend a ball held by the MacNeil. They knock on the door and are let in. They eat, drink, and play music all evening. MacNeil's trumpeter climbs the ramparts and proclaim: "Hear, ye people, and listen! The great MacNeil of Barra has dined, now all the princes of the earth are at liberty to dine." There is great feasting and dancing. Waving goodbye the couple finally leave the castle, rowing back to the shore.

Caisteal Chiosamul
(Kismul Castle)
(A Modern Hebridean Dance)

An Ceòl: The March *Father John MacMillan of Barra.*
Tempo: 34 Bars per minute. Crotchet = 68 per minute.
Time: 2/4, 8-Bar Introduction. 16 Bars to each step.
Count: 2 Counts to each Bar.

Na Comharraichean — NOTES

Caisteal Chiosamul is designed to be performed by any number of persons, i.e. solo, twasome, threesome..... We have here chosen to present the dance as a twasome — and perhaps this is the best way to perform the dance. If performed with uneven numbers of dancers, i.e. 1, 3, 5 and so on, the parts involving two dancers co-operating — the second and fourth steps — the sole dancer performs the movements as if dancing with a partner.

An Ceòl / Music — The dance was written to the March *Father John MacMillan of Barra* and the steps are designed to go with the music.

Gluasadan sònraichte — SPECIAL MOVEMENTS

Ball of foot is used unless otherwise stated.
Shuffles or **Treble Shuffles**
Spread
Shakes — From 5th Pos. RF is extended to 4th Int. Aer. Pos. (and); brought back a little before being extended fully to a 4th Int. Aer. Pos. High (a). The landing of the hop LF in this movement occurs simultaneously as RF reaches it highest point on count 'a'. The Shakes should be made as high as possible, but not over knee level, and strongly accented without being stiff in the movement. (Count 'and a').

Briseadh — Break RF

Bars

5   Jump, landing with LF in 3rd Inverted Pos. (Flat) (1);
Swivel on R heel, bringing toes outward, while sliding LF to 3rd Rear Pos. (and);
Jump, landing with RF in 3rd Inverted Pos. (Flat) (2);
Swivel on L heel, bringing toes outward, while sliding RF to

3rd Rear Pos. (and)
(Finish with both feet flat on the ground). This should be a smooth and easy movement. Slide feet on the ground. There is a slight sideways movement during the swivel.

6   Assemble RF in 3rd Pos. (3); Spread both feet towards 2nd Pos. with slightly bent knees (and);
Assemble RF in 3rd Pos. again (4). (A slight pause may occur during the 'Spread'.)
Finish with RF extended to 4th Midway Pos. Low

7   With a spring RF, Shuffle LF (5 and); Spring LF, Inward Brush RF to 3rd Pos., Raise RF to 3rd Aer. Pos. (6 and).
Or Double or Treble Shuffles for the MEN (only).
(Count: 5 and and a 6 and and a).

8   With RF in 3rd Aer. Pos. execute a round-the-leg action to 3rd Rear Aer. Pos.;
Spring RF, LF, RF, execute three Backstep Movements, finishing with LF in 3rd Aer. Pos.
(7 and 8).
Count: 1 and 2 and, 3 and 4, 5 and 6 and, 7 and 8
Obair nan Làmh / Handwork — Hands clasped together behind body.

Briseadh — Break LF
Same as above, but danced contra.

Tòiseachadh — INTRODUCTION
Bars

Couple stand, facing the front, the lady on the gent's left.

1 - 4   Stand with Head, Arms and Feet in Hebridean Starting Pos. Count - 1 2, 3 4, 5 6, 7 8.

5 - 8   Step to the Right (1), closing LF in front (2), Bow and Curtsey (Dèan modh) slowly (3 4, 5 6), step back to original positions (7 8).

A' chiad cheum — FIRST STEP
'Rowing out to the Castle'

Bars

Travel straight forward and then back during the first 4 Bars:

1   With a step RF forward in 4th Pos. (1);
Close LF behind in 3rd Rear Pos. (and);
Step RF forward in 4th Pos. (2);
A slight Hop on RF when passing LF through from rear to
4th Pos. lifting the foot slightly off the ground and with a
develope action bringing it forward.
The LF should 'almost' touch the R leg at the inner side in
a low 3rd (Rear) Acr. Pos. (and).

FIOS / NOTE: This is almost like a Scottish Country Dance Strathspey
Travelling Step but higher on toes and more stepping forward
than gliding.

2   Repeat Bar 1 with LF. Finish with RF in a very Low 3rd Rear
     Aer Pos. off the leg. (and)
     Count: 1 and 2 and, 3 and 4 and
   Obair nan Làmh / Handwork: Both hands clenched. Place LH
     over RH and make a rowing action on your right during Bar 1.
     Change places of hands R over L) and make a rowing action
     to your left during Bar 2.

3 - 4   Step RF back in 4th Rear Pos. to begin, move backwards with
     the Travel Step described above, back to your starting
     position. Finish with RF closed in 3rd Pos.
     Count: 5 and 6 and, 7 and 8 and
   Obair nan Làmh / Handwork: Both hands are clenched. Hold
     them together, thumbs and forefingers touching. Make rowing
     actions bringing hands down and forward, up and backwards
     towards body and then again. One movement to each step
     travelling backwards. Like rowing a boat.

5 - 8   BREAK RF — Briseadh.

9 - 12   Step LF forward to begin. Repeat Bars 1 - 4 contra.

13-16   BREAK LF — Briseadh.

An dara ceum — SECOND STEP
'Treble Step' or 'Knock on the Door — Open the Door and Welcome in'

Bars
1 - 2   With a Hop LF, lift RF up behind **off** L leg (1); Treble RF,
     i.e., Brush RF out-in, in 4th Int. Pos.
     Step RF in 3rd Pos. (and and a), then beat LF in 3rd Rear Pos.
     (2); slight pause that goes with the music (-);
     Treble RF out-in in 4th Int. Pos. (and and);
     Spring RF in place and lift LF up behind **off** L leg (3);
     Treble LF, i.e., Brush LF out-in, in 4th Int. Pos., Step LF in
     3rd Pos. (and and a), then beat RF in 3rd Rear Pos.(4);
     slight pause (-);
     Treble LF out-in in 4th Int. Pos. (and and).
     Count: 1 and and a 2 - and and, 3 and and a 4 - and and

Obair nan Làmh / Handwork — R Hand is clenched, L arm is hanging by the side; Make 3 knocks on the door action with R Hand during Bar 1. Open L Hand and bring from the side in a sweeping gesture in front of you, hand coming towards body (as a door being opened). R arm is hanging by the side during this movement on the 2nd Bar.

3 - 4 Spring LF in place. lifting RF up behind **off** L leg. (5);
Treble RF out-in, in 4th Int. Pos.;
Step RF in 3rd Pos. then beat LF in 3rd Rear Pos.
(and and a 6);
Treble RF out-in, in 4th Int. Pos.;
Step RF in 3rd Rear Pos. then beat LF in 3rd Pos. (and and a 7); Treble RF out-in, in
4th Int. Pos.; Beat RF in 3rd Pos. then beat LF in 3rd Rear Pos. (and and a 8).
Treble RF out-in, in 4th Int. Pos. (RF finishes on floor in 4th Int.Pos.) (and and).
Count: 5 and and a 6 and and, a 7 and and a 8 and and

 Obair nan Làmh / Handwork: L arm is hanging by the side, while R hand is open and is brought in front of body to the side and behind in a 'Welcome in' gesture. The movement should be slow and even and last through the 2 Bars.

 FIOS / NOTE: (A) In this step it is essential for the dancer to listen to the music and dance with it. The music tells you when to do slight pauses and drag the movements out.
(B) The Treble movement in this dance is a traditional Hornpipe movement, and is similar to the 'Shuffles' practised in the Scottish version of *The Sailors' Hornpipe.*

5 - 8 BREAK RF — Briseadh.

9 -12 Begin Hop RF, bringing LF up behind. Repeat Bars 1 - 4 contra, moving forward as you are now entering the castle.

 Obair nan Làmh / Handwork: Couple put their arms about their partners shoulder. They stay close until having to break apart for the Break.

13 - 16 BREAK LF, retiring back to place — Briseadh.

An treas ceum — THIRD STEP
'The Drinking Step'

Bars

1 Hopping on LF twice, making a Toe and Heel Movement with RF in 5th Pos. (or 4th Int. Pos. alternatively) with bent knee and foot well turned out (1 and);
Hop LF, bringing RF to 3rd Aer. Pos. (2);
Spring RF in place, as a Backstep, bringing LF to 3rd Aer. Pos (and);

2 Hopping on RF four times, extend LF to 4th Int. Aer. Pos. High (3); Bring LF in to 3rd Aer. Pos. (and);
Extend LF again to a 4th Int. Aer. Pos. High (4); Bring LF again in to 3rd Aer. Pos. (and).
The extensions should be sharp and the body is leaning slightly backward.

3 - 4 With a Hop on RF to begin, Repeat Bars 1 - 2 contra.
Count: 1 and 2 and, 3 and 4 and, 5 and 6 and, 7 and 8 and
Obair nan Làmh / Handwork: Head is tilted backwards (look up). Palms towards your face, hold them as if drinking out of a horn. R hand close to the mouth and L hand in the air. You drink from the thin end of the horn and hold the thick end in your left hand. As when emptying a real horn you have to lean more backwards as the step proceeds.

Variation: Hold the imaginary drinking horn in front of you while doing the toe-heel movement, then drink, increasing the angle of the head during the 'kicks.'

5 - 8 BREAK RF — Briseadh.

9 -12 Hop on RF to begin, repeat Bars 1 - 4 contra.

13-16 BREAK LF — Briseadh.

An ceathramh ceum — FOURTH STEP
'Trumpeting Step'

Bars

During Bars 1 - 4 the dancers describe a complete turn clockwise on the spot.

1 - 2   With a Hop on LF, place RF in Inverted 2nd Pos. (1);
Place RF on Heel in Forward 2nd Pos.
(NO HOP) (and); Beat LF in place (2);
Step RF on ball in Forward 2nd Pos. (and); place LF on
Heel in Forward 2nd Pos. (3); Step RF in place (and); Step LF
in 2nd Pos. on Ball. (4).
Count: 1 and 2 and, 3 and 4 [Hop—heel—beat—step—
step— step—step]

3 - 4   Continuing turning clockwise. With a Hop on RF to begin, repeat Bars 1-2 contra.
Count: 5 and 6 and, 7 and 8

Obair nan Làmh / Handwork — Head is tilted back, look up. Both hands are clenched and held in front of the mouth as blowing a trumpet. R Hand nearest the mouth.

5 - 8   BREAK RF — Briseadh.

9 -12   Turning anti-clockwise on the spot, repeat Bars 1- 4 contra.

13 - 16   BREAK LF — Briseadh.

An còigeamh ceum — FIFTH STEP
'The Polka'

Bars

Obair nan Làmh / Handwork — Couple facing one another. Man places his hands on partners shoulders. Woman holds man on the waist. Open up to face front at end of the 4th Bar.

1 - 4   With 4 Travelling Steps as described in the First Step (Woman starting with LF moving backwards and Man starting with RF moving forward);
Dance around forward and round (clockwise) to the left.
Travelling approx. 1/4 on each step.
Open up to face front at end of 4th step.
Count: 1 and 2 and, 3 and 4 and, 5 and 6 and 7 and 8 and

5 - 8   BREAK RF — Briseadh.

9 - 12   Dance around again. Man starts LF moving backwards,
          Woman with RF moving forward.
          Circle around backwards to the right (clockwise) back to
          places and open up to face front at end of Bar 4.

13 - 16   BREAK LF — Briseadh.

FIOS / NOTE: The dancing around can also, as an alternative, be treated in
          a more Polka-like fashion, not dancing round in a strict circle, but
          still done with the travelling steps.

An t-siathamh ceum — SIXTH STEP
'Waving Goodbye'

Bars

1 Dance 2 Rocks: Spring on to RF, placing LF in 5th Rear Pos. (1);
Spring on to LF, placing RF in 5th Pos. (and).;
Lift RF up to 3rd Aer. Pos. and round-the-leg to 3rd Rear Aer. Pos. (a);
Spring RF and LF execute 2 Back Steps (2 and). Finish with RF in 3rd Aer. Pos.

2 Done moving sideways slightly to the right: With a Spring on to RF, point LF in 5th Pos. (3);
Hop RF, extending LF with a Shake to a 4th Int. Aer. Pos. High (and a); Hop RF, pointing LF in 5th Pos. (4);
Hop RF, extending LF with a Shake to a 4th Int. Aer. Pos. High (and a).
Count: 1 and a 2 and, 3 and a 4 and a

Obair nan Làmh / Handwork: Hands are clasped together behind body on Bar 1. On the 2nd Bar, left arm hangs by the side while, in unison with the Shakes, R hand waves Goodbye diagonally out to the right.

3 - 4   With a Spring on to LF, placing RF in 5th Rear Pos., to begin, repeat Bars 1 - 2 contra, moving slightly to the left.
Count: 5 and a 6 and, 7 and a 8 and a

5 - 8   BREAK RF — Briseadh.

9 -12   Spring LF to begin, repeat Bars 1 - 4 contra, moving sideways during the shakes.

13-16   Break LF — Briseadh.

An t-seachdamh ceum — SEVENTH STEP
'Rowing back to the shore'

Bars
1 -16   Repeat the 1st Step once more.

A' Chrìoch — FINISH
Step to 2nd Pos. on RF, Close LF to RF in Hebridean 1st Pos. (flat) and Bow and Curtsey — Dèan modh.

100

Cath nan Coileach
(A traditional reel)

An Ceòl: *Boc Liath nan Gobhar* also known as *Cath nan Coileach.*
Tempo: 60 Bars per minute for the Slow Part.
          Crotchet — 120 per minute.
          75-80 Bars per minute for the Quick Part.
          Crotchet — 160 per minute.
Time: 6/8.
Count: 2 Counts to each Bar.

'S e dannsa cheathrar no dà chupal a tha seo. Mas e cupail a tha a' dannsa tha an nighean air làimh-dheis a' ghille. Tha am port mall aig an toiseach agus a' fàs gu math nas luaithe na ceòl ruidhle. Tha na gluasadan a' sealltanin mar a bhiodh na coilich a' cogadh air a chèile, mun tòisicheadh an t-sabaid.

Cath nan Coileach — 'The Cockfight' is a dance for four people or two couples if so preferred. If danced by couples the girl is on her partner's right. The dance is divided in to two distictive parts — one danced slightly slower than normal reel tempo and the other much faster. The sequences are repeated as often as desired.

The movements of the dance is said to represent the circling of fighting cocks before the actual combat.

The tune played for this dance is *Boc Liath nan Gobhar* which translates to *The Shaggy Grey Buck*, which is a well-known pipe-jig. Pipers on the Isle of Barra often know this tune as *Cath nan Coileach.*

Na Comharraichan — NOTES

Obair nan Làmh / Handwork — All four dancers cross hands and join them in the middle, with the person facing, so that they stand in the form of a cross. This formation is retained throughout the dance.

Gluasadan sònraichte — SPECIAL MOVEMENTS

Ball of foot is used unless otherwise stated.

An Dannsa — THE DANCE

Slow Tempo

Bars

1 - 8   All dance 8 Pas de Basques moving from side to side. Start with a R Pas de Basque.

9 - 16   Dance 8 Skip Change of Step clockwise round, not necessarily finishing in your original position.

Quick Tempo

1 - 8   Dance 8 Ceum cùl dùbailte on the spot.

9 - 16   Spinning round clockwise, not necessarily finishing in your original position, using a pivot step. i.e: Stepping on to the RF and pushing off with the LF, repeated 16 times.

This sequence of 16 Bars Slow Tempo and 16 Bars Quick Time is repeated as many times as desired.

Ruidhle nan Coileach Dhubha
(A traditional reel)

An Ceòl: *Ruidhle nan Coileach Dhubha.*
Tempo: 52 Bars per minute. Crotchet — 104 per minute.
Time: 2/4.
Count: 2 Counts to each Bar.

'S e dannsa Gàidhlig a tha seo, air a shuidheachadh a rèir nan seann ruidhle-cearcaill a bh' air an cleachdadh anns na h-Eileanan. Bhiodh dà chupal a' danns' ann an cearcall agus a' seatadh air a spot, mu seach. 'S e port-a-beul dhen aon ainm no am port air a chluich air a' phìob mhòr an ceòl tha leis an dannsa.

Ruidhle nan Coileach Dhubha — The Blackcocks' Reel is a reel for four people performed to the dance-song of the same name. Accompaniment to this dance was traditionally sung — puirt-a-beul — or played on the pipes. The words of the song are —

Ruidhlidh na coilich dhubha	Reeled the blackcocks
's dannsaidh na tunnagan,	and danced the ducks,
Ruidhlidh na coilich dhubha	Reeled the blackcocks
Air a' bhruthaich shìos ud.	on the banks up there.

The dance involves a mime of 'blackcocks' and 'ducks'. The dancing couple are the 'blackcocks' while the kneeling couple are the 'ducks'. This dance, as well as 'Cath nan Coileach,' is probably based on or a variation and extension of the old circular reel of the islands, which involves two couples circling and setting on the spot in turns.

Na Comharraichean — NOTES

Obair nan Làmh / Handwork — When the dancer **sets, kneels or dance around one another** arms are raised in 3rd Pos. and fingers are snapped in time with the music. i.e. all the time but for the circle. Hands are held at shoulder height for the circle.

If danced by couples the girl should be on her partner's right. When kneeling, the dancer goes down on the left knee.

Gluasadan sònraichte — SPECIAL MOVEMENTS

Ball of foot is used unless otherwise stated.

Skips — Hop LF, Step RF forward (and 1); Hop RF, Step LF forward (and 2); repeated as desired.

Tòiseachadh — INTRODUCTION

Bars

1 - 4   The dancers stand in a line and dance on after one another to form a circle. Use Skips to enter beginning with the RF. Finish facing in.

An Dannsa — THE DANCE

Bars

5 - 8   All dance 8 Ceum cùl dùbailte on the spot facing the opposite person.

9 - 12   Dancers 1 and 3 kneel down while Dancers 2 and 4 keep on setting with 8 Ceum cùl dùbailte.

13 - 16 Dancers 2 and 4 kneel down while Dancers 1 and 3 set.

17 - 20 Dancers 1 with 2 and 3 with 4 change places with 2 Skip Change of Steps giving Right shoulder.
Set in new position with 4 Ceum cùl dùbailte, facing back from where you came.

21 - 24 Repeat Bars 17 - 20 going back to original places.

25 - 28 Dancers 1 and 3 change places with 2 Skip Change of Steps giving Right shoulders;
then set with 4 Ceum cùl dùbailte facing in.

Dancers 2 and 4 set on spot with 8 Ceum cùl dùbailte, facing in.

29 - 32	Dancers 2 and 4 change places with 2 Skip Change of Steps giving Right shoulders; then set with 4 Ceum cùl dùbailte facing in.

Dancers 1 and 3 set on spot with 8 Ceum cùl dùbailte, facing in.

33 - 40	Repeat Bars 25 - 32 so that all return to original places.

41 - 44	Dancers 1 and 3 change places with 2 Skip Change of Steps giving Right shoulders; then change back to own place giving Right shoulders, 2 Skip Change of Step.

Dancers 2 and 4 set on spot with 8 Ceum cùl dùbailte, facing in.

45 - 48	Dancers 2 and 4 change places with 2 Skip Change of Steps giving Right shoulders; then change back to own place giving Right shoulders, 2 Skip Change of Step.

Dancers 1 and 3 set on spot with 8 Ceum cùl dùbailte, facing in.

49 - 56	All join hands and circle round clockwise with 8 skip Change of Steps.

57 -	Release the circle and dance off on a line with Skips.

Dannsa nan Sgoiltean Beaga
(A modern reel on traditional basis)

An Ceòl: *Cuir Sa Chiste Mhòir Mi — Put Me in the Great Chest.*
Tempo: 56 Bars per minute. Crotchet — 112 per minute.
Time: 2/4, 8-Bar Introduction.
Count: 2 Counts to each Bar.

Chaidh an dannsa seo a chur ri chèile le Ceit Anna NicFhionghuin agus clann a clas nuair a bha Comhairle Nan Eilean a' bagairt sgoiltean beaga an eilein a dhùnadh. Tha na steapan a' sealltainn mar a bha na daoine air iorram sìos is suas gu Steòrnabhagh, agus tha maoidheadh nan dòrn a' samhlachadh fearg nan daoine an aghaidh na Comhairle.

This Reel was devised by Katie Ann Mackinnon and the schoolchildren of the Isle of Barra as a mean of protest upon the suggested closing of a number of small island schools.

Dannsa an Sgoiltean Beaga means 'The Dance of the Small Schools'.

The dance shows how people travelled around the islands and to Stornoway pleading for the schools to remain open. The shaking of fists represents the defiance of the small schools and their fighting spirit to remain open. At the end of the dance two schools stays open while one, unfortunately, was closed.

Na Comharraichean — NOTES

Obair nan Làmh / Handwork — When the dancer sets with Ceum cùl dùbailte arms are raised to 3rd Pos. and the fingers snapped in time with the music. In the Hop-Heel-Close-Beat the fist on the working side is shaken diagonally forward and the other hand is held at the waist (as in 1st Pos.). Whenever turning or holding hands, they are held at shoulder height.

Gluasadan sònraichte — SPECIAL MOVEMENTS

Ball of foot is used unless otherwise stated.

Hop-Heel-Close-Beat — Hop LF (and); Step RF on Heel towards
4th Int. Pos. (1); Close LF to 3rd Rear Pos. (and); Beat RF in 3rd Pos. (2).
Repeat with LF contra (and 3 and 4).
Count: and 1 and 2, and 3 and 4

Obair nan Làmh / Handwork — When doing the movement with RF,
shake Right fist diag. fwd in time with the music. Left hand at waist (as in
1st Pos.). Shake Left fist when doing the movement on the LF.

Tòiseachadh — INTRODUCTION

Bars

1 - 4   The dancers stand in a line of three in Hebridean Starting
         Position, holding hands at shoulder height, side dancers
         holding their skirts with their free hand. All facing the front.
         Count: 1 2, 3 4, 5 6, 7 8

5 - 8   All Bow slowly — Dèan modh — and then point their RF
         forward ready to begin.
         Count: 1 2, 3 4, 5 6, 7 8

First Figure

Bars

1 - 4   All three dance 2 Skip Change straight forward (and 1 and 2,
         and 3 and 4); then retiré back to place with 4 Ceum cùl
         dùbailte, stepping on to RF, LF, RF, LF
         (and 5 and 6 and 7 and 8).

5 - 8   Repeat Bars 1 - 4.

Second Figure

Bars

1 - 4   Dancer 1 and 2 turn once round with Right hand (shoulder height) with 4 Skip Change of Steps; while Dancer 3 faces them and dances 8 Ceum cùl dùbailte on the spot, stepping on to RF to begin.

              Dancer 3 raises hands to 3rd Pos. and snaps her fingers in time with the music, whilst setting.

5 - 8   Dancer 2 and 3 turn once round with Left hand, 4 Skip Change of Steps, while Dancer 1 sets on the spot with 8 Ceum cùl dùbailte, RF, LF; snapping her fingers.

Third Figure

Bars

1 - 8   Repeat the First Figure, but contra. i.e. start with the Skip Change on the LF.

Fourth Figure
Bars

1 - 8   Repeat the Second Figure contra. i.e. on Bars 1 - 4 Dancers 2
         and 3 turns Right hand while
         Dancer 1 sets; and on Bars 5 - 8, Dancers 1 and 2 turns Left
         hand while Dancer 3 sets.

Fifth Figure
Bars

1 - 4   Dancers 1 and 3 (sides) face the middle, raising their hands to
         3rd Pos. and snapping their fingers in time with the music:
         dance 8 Ceum cùl dùbilte on the spot, starting stepping on
         to RF to begin.
         Dancer 2 (middle): Dance Hop-Heel-Close-Beat with RF
         and LF, shaking her fists accordingly to Right and Left. (and
         1 and 2, and 3 and 4);
         She then retirés back to place with 4 Ceum cùl-dùbailte,
         stepping on to RF, LF, RF, LF (and 5 and 6 and 7
         and 8)

5 - 8   Dancers 1 and 3 face forward and repeat what Dancer 2 did
         on bars 1-4;
         while Dancer 2 dance 8 Ceum cùl dùbailte on the spot,
         RF, LF
         Dancer 1 starting with **RF** and Dancer 3 with **LF** i.e.
         executing the step outwards from the middle.

Sixth Figure
Bars

1 - 6   Reel of Three: Dancers 1 and 2 give right shoulder to begin
         and Dancer 3 go to the right to begin the Reel.
         All return to places.

7 - 8   All dance 4 Ceum cùl dùbailte on the spot, facing the front
         RF, LF, RF. LF.

Seventh Figure

Bars

1 - 8   Repeat the Sixth Figure contra. Dancer 2 and 3 begin the Reel giving Left shoulder and Dancer 1 goes to her Left to enter.

Eight Figure

Bars

1 - 4   All dance Three hands across with Right hands at shoulder height for 4 Skip Change of Steps.

5 - 7   Three hands across with Left hands at shoulder height for 2 Skip Change of Steps.
(and 1 and 2 and 3 and 4) All return to original places with 2 Ceum cùl dùbailte, RF and LF
(and 5 and 6).

8   Finish pose: Dancers 1 and 3 (sides) Step to the Right and Curtsey — Dèan modh.

Dancer 2 (middle) place R Heel in 4th Int. Pos. and lifts Right fist in defiance and Step LF in 3rd Rear Pos. while shaking Right fist.

An Ceòl / Music

The music for these dances may be found in the following books as listed per dance:

Tulach Gorm / Tulloch Gorm is known in various settings for the Pipes:
> P.M. W. Ross's Collection of Highland Bagpipe Music, Book 1.
> Scots Guards Standard Setting of Pipe Music, 1954.
> The Glendaruel Collection, Bagpipe Music, compiled by
> P.M. W. Norris.
> The Gordon Highlanders, Pipe Music Collection, Vol I.
> Standard Settings of Pipe Music of The Seaforth Highlanders,
> 1936.
> Ross's Collection of Pipe Music, William Ross, 1885.
>> These six all being titled *Tulloch Gorm*.
> Logan's Complete Collection of Highland Bagpipe Music,
> Tutor No. 4.
>> This one being titled *Tulloch Gorum*.

Over the Water to Charlie is included in 'Standard Settings of Pipe Music of The Seaforth Highalnders,' 1936, where it is styled as a 6/8 March; and in 'Queen's Own Highlanders (Seaforth and Camerons) Standard Settings of Pipe Music,' where it is also styled as a 6/8 March.

Highland Laddie is a very common Pipe tune, and often used as *Salute to the Chieftain*. It is set as a 2/4 March.
> Queen's Own Highlanders (Seaforth and Camerons) Standard
> Settings of Pipe Music.
> The Army Manual of Bagpipe Tunes and Drum Beatings, Army
> Piping Committee, Book 2.
> Logan's Complete Tutor for the Highland Bagpipe, Revised by
> J.A. MacLellan.
> The College of Piping Highland Bagpipe Tutor, Part I, College of
> Piping, Glasgow.
> The S.P.B.A. Tutor and Text Book, Vol. I, Glasgow, 1962.
> Pipe Major Gray's and Drum Major Seton's Bagpipe and Drum
> Tutors, Tutor #1.

The Glenallen Collection of Bagpipe Music, P.M. W. Norris, Glasgow.
Ross's Collection of Pipe Music, William Ross, 1885. Reprinted 1976.
Scots Guards Standard Setting of Pipe Music, 1954, 4th Edition.
The Cabar Feidh Collection, Pipe Music of the Queen's Own Highlanders (Seaforth and Camerons). — (Hielan' Laddie, Reel, 4/4, Sett. by P.M. I. Morrison).

Blue Bonnets is a rather common 6/8 march as set for the Pipes:
> *All the Blue Bonnets:*

The SPBA Tutor and Text Book Vol. 1, 1962.
> *All the Blue Bonnets are over the Border:*

Logan's Collection of Highland Bagpipe Music, Revised ED. by P.M. W. Ross.
Logan's Complete Collection of Highland Bagpipe Music, Tutor No. 1.
Standard Settings of Pipe Music of The Seaforth Highlanders, 1936.
Ross's Collection of Pipe Music, William Ross, 1885.
Scots Guards Standard Settings of Pipe Music, 1954.
> *Blue Bonnets:*

Queen's Own Highlanders (Seaforth and Camerons) Standard Settings of Pipe Music.
The Piper's Delight, Arr. and Ed. by P.M. Robert Reid.
The College of Piping Highland Bagpipe Tutor, Part 1.
The Bagpipe, A Complete Tutor with a selection of Irish and Scottish Tunes, P.M. Bill Cleary, 1982.

Scotch Measure was performed to the tune/song *The Twa Bonnie Maidens*, and in pipe music it is represented by the tune *Prince Charlie's Welcome to Skye*, and it is also similar to the well-known march *Dornoch Links*.
> *Prince Charlie's Welcome to Skye* can be found in:

Logan's Complete Collection of Highland Bagpipe Music, Tutor No. 1.
Ross's Collection of Pipe Music, William Ross, 1885.
> *Dornoch Links* can be found in:

The Glenallan Collection, A New Coll. of Bagpipe Music,
P.M. W, Norris.
Logan's Collection of Highland Bagpipe Music. Rev. Ed. by
P.M. W. Ross.
Scots Guards Standard Settings of Pipe Music, Vol. II.
Logan's Complete Collection of Highland Bagpipe Music,
Tutor No. 1.
Queen's Own Highlanders (Seaforth & Camerons) Standard
Settings of Pipe Music.
The Gordon Highlanders, Pipe Music Collection, Vol. I.
Standard Settings of Pipe Music of the Seaforth Highlanders,
1936.

The tunes running with **Aberdonian Lassie / Till A-rithist** are the 6/8
Marches *The Quaker* and the very similar tune the *The Quaker's Wife*.
Either fits the dance to perfection.

Quaker's Wife: Standard Settings of Pipe Music of the Seaforth
Highlanders, 1936.
Queen's Own Highlanders (Seaforth & Camerons) Standard
Settings of Pipe Music.
The Quaker: Pipe Major Donald MacLeod's Collection of Music
for the Highland Bagpipe, Vol. 5.
Logan's Complete Collection of Highland Bagpipe Music,
Tutor No. 3.

Flowers of Edinburgh is found as a 4/4 March in:
Bagpipe Music for Dancing,, compiled by Captain John A.
MacLellan, M.B.E.

Miss Forbes. The tune used today for this dance is *The Wee Man at the Loom*
which can be found in the 'Queen's Own Highlanders (Seaforth & Camerons)
Standard Settings of Pipe Music,' as a 2/4 March. D.G. MacLennan give in his
book the music of a tune called *Miss Forbes*, but which is of a totally different
structure compared to *The Wee Man at the Loom*.
Miss Forbes' Farewell to Banff as a 2/4 March or Quickstep can be found in:

The Seumas MacNeill Collection of Bagpipe Music, College of
Piping, Glasgow.

The Seumas MacNeill Collection of Bagpipe Music, Book 1.
Logan's Complete Collection of Highland Bagpipe Music,
Tutor No. 5.
Ross's Collection of Pipe Music, W. Ross, 1885.

The tune for **Caisteal Chiosamul** was devised for *(Father) John MacMillan of Barra*, and is a 2/4 March composed by Norman MacDonald. It can be found in :
Pipe Major Donald MacLeod's Collection of Music for the
Highland Bagpipe, Vol. 1, Glasgow.

Cuir Sa Chiste Mhòir Mi — Put Me in the Great Chest, a Reel. This tune was originally included in Angus MacKay's 'Piper's Assistant' 1840 where it goes by its Gaelic title. The great chest in question is a coffin. The story goes that as the composer of this fine tune lay on his death bed he asked for a last bottle of stout. He finished it and requested that the bedroom window be opened."I will throw this empty bottle and wherever it lands is where I wish my final resting place to be." He missed the window and was buried on top of the wardrobe!

HEBRIDEAN DANCING OUTFIT

The outfit adopted by **Bòrd Dannsa nan Eileanach** in 1987 is, from that time, the accepted outfit to be worn for the purpose of displaying such dances as have been set out in this book.

The dress for women:
BLOUSE
White cotton or similar, having short puffed sleeves with ruffle edge, also of white cotton or similar. The neck-line has a stand-up ruffle of 1/2 inch matching the sleeve ruffle. The blouse has front button opening and a collar.

SKIRT
Striped cotton or similar lightweight material. Colour is optional but a stripe must be predominant in the material. The skirt is very full, (3 yrds for teenage/adult size), gathered at the waist and with 1-1 1/2 inch waistband. Overall length of skirt is calf-length. The skirt is worn over a very full white underskirt of white cotton or similar. The underskirt should be at least knee-lenght.

The skirt is lifted over the right knee and the hemline is fastened to the waistband. The fold should sit in a triangle flowing to the hemline to left and right.

CAPE / PLAID
Self-coloured to match stripe in skirt and of lightweight material (wool/mixed). It is gathered at the neckline leaving at least 2 inches from the edge at either side without gather, to sit on the shoulders. The cape is knee-lenght to the back and the 3 edges are fringed to the depth of 1/2 inch. The neckline has a 1 1/2 inch tie which is crossed at the front under the collarline of the blouse and held to the blouse with a brooch.

SHAWL
A knitted shawl to match the general colour of the skirt in the island fashion

HOSE
White socks, knee-length for children and tights of matching colour to cape and skirt for teenagers and adults.

The dress for men:

The man should wear the kilt, any tartan may be worn. Plain knitted hose. Day-wear sporran and belt. The shirt should be of the round-necked type, sometimes called 'folklore' or 'colonial' type of shirt. No tie should be worn. Bonnet may be worn if desired.

Shoes for Men and Women

Today Highland Dancing Pumps should be worn; preferable black.

Dress in the old days:

Traditionally the male dress for dancing these dances would have been ordinary day wear. The footwear would have been ordinary boots. trousers, a knitted fisherman's jersey and perhaps a Tam O' Shanter. The girls would have worn their ordinary shoes with quite a high heel.

——o0o——

Eideadh nam Boireannach

Blousa geal cotain le muilichinnean sìos gun uileann. Coileir mu òirleach a dh'àird agus putain sìos an aghaidh.

Sgiorta pailt striopach de chotan no clòimh bhog. Dath dorcha ged a dh'fhaodas na striopan a bhith de dhath sam bith. Feumaidh e bhith mu shia oirlich fon ghlùin — an t-iomal air a thogail air an taobh cheart agus air a chur 's a bhann le prìne.

Ploid aon-dathach de dhath shrip an sgiorta agus den aon aodach. Tha e truisde aig an amhaich ann am bann, mu leud òirleach gu leth, a fàgail dà òirleach dhan aodach air gach taobh gu laighe air gach gualainn. Tha sia òirlich a bharrachd dhen bhann air fhàgail air gach taobh, gus a dhol tarsainn air a chèile aig an uchd 's air a cheangal ris a bhlousa le broidse.

Stocainnean tiughe àrd an aon dath ris a' phloid.

Brògan dannsa no casan-rùisgte.

Eideadh nam Fear

Fèileadh de bhreacan sam bith. Lèine seann fhasanta gun choileir.

Stocainnean-glùineadh aon-dathach.

Brògan dannsa no casan rùisgte.

——oOo——

117